Strength in the Shadow

THE IMPOSSIBLE MADE POSSIBLE

Lisa J. Lancaster

TRILOGY CHRISTIAN PUBLISHERS

TUSTIN, CA

Trilogy Christian Publishers
A Wholly Owned Subsidiary of Trinity Broadcasting Network
2442 Michelle Drive
Tustin, CA 92780

For information, address Trilogy Christian Publishing

Rights Department, 2442 Michelle Drive, Tustin, Ca 92780.

Trilogy Christian Publishing/ TBN and colophon are trademarks of Trinity Broadcasting Network.

For information about special discounts for bulk purchases, please contact Trilogy Christian Publishing.

Manufactured in the United States of America

10 9 8 7 6 5 4 3 2 1

Library of Congress Cataloging-in-Publication Data is available.
ISBN 978-1-64773-794-8
ISBN 978-1-64773-795-5 (ebook)

Contents

Dedication

I dedicate this book to my husband, Jeff Lancaster. Words are not enough to convey my gratitude, respect, and love for a man who laid down his life and gave all he had to help me live through the valley of the shadow of death. His genuine love, unwavering faith, endless work, creative solutions to so many problems, and commitment to me often have me at a loss for words. I love you, Jeff, and one day you will see our Beloved and hear Him say, "Well done, good and faithful servant."

Preface

This journey through the valley of the shadow of death was one that I never expected to have, but it nevertheless changed the course of my life for good. Walking through the valley of the shadow of death and out to the other side, I was strengthened and discovered how to *carry presence* and *live possible*.

To those who see themselves with no hope, no strength, and no future: may the words of the testimony in this book breathe life into you, strengthen you to rise up out of your sickbed, allow you to see the hand to help you out of the pit, and release you from the prison in your mind. To those of you caring for a sick loved one: may you find comfort, hope, and strength in this testimony and believe that all things are possible with God.

With men this is impossible, but with God all things are possible.

Matthew 19:26 (NKJV)

Acknowledgements

To all the people who took the time to write letters of testimony for this book, you have my sincere thanks, appreciation, and love.

Thank you, Yonnah Ben-Levy, for painting an original work of art for the cover of this book. I so appreciate your kindness, love, and beautiful works of art.

Thank you to all my family and friends who earnestly prayed for us all those years in the valley. I am forever grateful you are in my life. I love you all.

To our five children, Cody and his wife Haley, Christina, Chelsea, Tyler and his wife Austyn, and Brannigan: thank you for loving your dad and I and not giving up on us in those difficult years. We love you.

To our nine grandchildren for bringing us so much joy: Grandpa and Grammy love you all!

Thank you to Jeshu and Teresa Ram, presidents of Impact Asia International, in gratitude for giving us an opportunity to share our story in India and being such an encouragement to us.

Thank you to Pastor Debbie Dundas for fanning the flame and for all the prayer and love covering over us all! We love you!

Thank you to Dr. Paul T. McBride for staying the course in trying to cure me and helping my family and I in the darkest of days. All your efforts are greatly appreciated.

Thank you to all the pastors, prophets, and leaders who so fervently prayed for my healing all those years. My heart is so full of gratitude for your faithfulness in speaking truth and declaring the Word of God.

Special Thanks

Special thanks to Pastor Toby Mitchell, Lead Pastor of Access Church, Spokane, Washington. Thank you so very much for all the words of encouragement and truth spoken to me. You encouraged me to speak, even if it was one word, and that meant everything! The time spent at your church so inspired me and helped bring this book to life! The verse the Lord said to share at Access Church is the cornerstone of this book's testimony. Thank you for imparting the Father's heart so well! Much love to you and Patty.

CHAPTER 1

Blindsided

Raising five children by the time I was twenty-four wasn't exactly how I had planned my life to be, but by the grace of God, each day was filled with many blessings. Thankfulness for life experiences that helped shape a hard work ethic, a can-do attitude, resiliency to overcome, and a whole lot of prayer carried me throughout each day.

Life was going along as most in 2007 with five children, working full-time for the government, serving in church, staying active, and managing the family's schedules. For the most part, I was healthy except for a nagging thyroid, which had to be checked frequently. In March, I went in for yet another thyroid scan and blood work, but this time, something changed. Along with feeling unusually tired, having difficulty swallowing, and my hair falling out, I was now having trouble concentrating, so I had to get checked out by a physician. Three doctors conferred together and decided the best course of action was to remove my thyroid. So, the referral went out to the endocrinologist for a thyroid removal consultation. My husband and I initially thought this would resolve the nagging problems that kept coming up in the last two years. The consultation went well, and the surgery to remove my thyroid was scheduled right away. At this point, I was on a road that consisted of several doctor visits every month.

Going in for major surgery, I had no red flags. I trusted the doctors who advised me that this was the best option, so off to St. Joseph Hospital, I went. I remember the surgical waiting room like it was yesterday. The curtains were all drawn, lights low, machines beeping, and yet there was a peaceful quietness in the room. Suddenly, a male nurse walked into my room. He just looked at me with the brightest, most loving eyes; he was wearing all white scrubs and had glistening blonde wavy hair. He spoke these words: "I am here for you." I looked right at him and said, "Okay." He spoke again with eyes locked on me, "I am here for you."

I pondered what was happening to me; I had this sense that something of profound importance was transpiring. Again, the words, "I am here for you," rang out into my room and pierced me right into my being. His voice echoed as I suddenly looked to my left, and my husband, Jeff, walked through the curtain. I had desperately wanted to see Jeff since the moment they brought me back to the presurgical suite. When I turned back around to speak to the nurse in white scrubs, he was gone. Now that Jeff was in the room with me and I was more at ease, I pondered what just took place. "Where did he go?" I asked Jeff. "Who?" he replied. "That male nurse in white scrubs that was just in here," I said. Jeff had a perplexed look on his face and did not know why I was adamant about finding the nurse. I kept asking about the nurse.

Just then, another nurse in blue scrubs came in and started working on the computer by my bed. I asked the nurse, "Where is the nurse that was just in here in white scrubs go?" The nurse in blue scrubs responded, "White scrubs?" I replied, "Yes, the male nurse with blonde hair and white scrubs." She paused and looked right at me and said in a stern voice, "There are no male nurses on this shift." She typed a few things and then departed out the curtain.

As I told my husband what the nurse in white scrubs had said to me, the curtains flew open, and there were two transport aides to take me to surgery. I told my husband, "I love you," and off I went. I remember nothing but peace and calmness until I abruptly woke up in pain in an unfamiliar hospital room with my husband at the bedside.

The doctor informed us that I had coded during the thyroidectomy and had stopped breathing, and that they briefly lost my heartbeat. Trying to process this near-death experience—well, for a minute, actual death—was a lot, but then the dreaded news came that no one ever wants to hear. The doctor told us I had cancer.

Yes, I bawled! My first thought was, *What about my kids? This cannot be happening.* I was a young mother, thirty-seven years old, and started a career five years earlier with the United States government. Cancer was nowhere on our radar, and never did it cross my mind that my husband and I would have to deal with something so devastating.

In that hospital room, it was a bit like *The Twilight Zone.* People were coming in and out; there were tests, tests, and more tests, and new, strange things being said and done to me that I never imagined. The nurses tried their very best to help, but nothing seemed to go as "normal" during the entire hospital stay. I was still wrapping my head around the doctor saying they "lost me for a second" when I was not breathing and briefly did not have a heartbeat.

The only thing I remember after leaving the surgical preparation room was feeling a sense of peace, like everything would be okay, even though everything in my body was screaming otherwise. The process of having your throat filleted wide open and a major organ being removed—delicately, as to not to cut my vocal cords, or I would have lost my ability to speak—is not fun. Later,

I was told by the doctor that they removed lymph nodes because they had to remove a mass from my thyroid bed. The process of removing drains from the neck is even worse than the actual thyroid removal procedure.

What made things even more horrendous was that no pain medications were administered during the procedure because the nurse-in-training who I agreed to let treat me forgot to give them to me. I screamed in horror as she slowly pulled with all her might to remove these giant tubes with teeth from deep inside my neck.

I am painting this picture because despite the absolute physical torment I experienced in my body, my faith did not change. I knew that God had me. I hurt, I was in terrible pain, I was scared of what was to come, and I didn't know why any of this was happening, but I was so thankful that I had faith.

Psalm 23 is a familiar passage of scripture to many people who look to it for strength in times of loss; for me this passage of scripture not only comforts but quickens life.

The Lord is my shepherd;
I shall not [lack].
He makes me lie down in green pastures;
He leads me beside the still waters.
He restores my soul;
He leads me in the paths of righteousness

5

For His name's sake.

Yea, though I walk through the valley of the shadow of death,

I will fear no evil;

For You are with me;

Your rod and Your staff, they comfort me.

You prepare a table before me in the presence of my enemies;

You anoint my head with oil;

My cup runs over.

Surely goodness and mercy shall follow me

All the days of my life;

And I will dwell in the house of The Lord

Forever.

Psalm 23:1-6 (NKJV)

This passage of the Bible would forever mark me in a way I never imagined. Now, I am no theologian, nor did I attend seminary. I was a primary school teacher before taking a public service position with the United States government. However, I love to study, and I would always read the Word of God, searching for more. What I found through reading the Word of God was faith.

This particular passage in Psalm 23 would play a key role in the darkest hours of my life. Not only had I just experienced physical death during surgery, but I also experienced the grace of God through an angel who spoke to me and demonstrated that God was with me in the dark, difficult places. Pondering the presence in the presurgical room, I realized the magnitude of the fact that I was not alone, that I did not need to be afraid nor fear the unknown, and that peace was available to me in terrible circumstances if I chose to receive it. I had more peace after having stopped breathing and my heart briefly stopping than I did before going into the hospital in the first place. I had found peace while in the midst of the storm.

The whole reason I agreed to surgery was because the doctors told me it would stop the crazy cycle of my thyroid crashing, which had been causing some huge and unexpected struggles. I would be driving my car home from work and suddenly have terrible brain fog, like I would forget where I was driving. I also would experience difficulty seeing, irregular heartbeats, horrid fatigue for no reason, losing my hair, a hugely swollen tongue that made it feel like I couldn't breathe, feeling insanely cold all the time, and losing my voice for no reason. That lovely cycle went on until I agreed to the surgery.

Prior to the surgery for a total thyroidectomy, the doctors had diagnosed me with severe Hashimoto's disease, an autoimmune-mediated thyroid condition followed by a diagnosis of a follicular variant papillary carcinoma—the kind of cancer you don't want, because it's aggressive and can return or show up anytime or anywhere. This ridiculous laundry list of symptoms demonstrated why I agreed to such an invasive surgery. The thyroid gland plays a major role in the body, so I was reluctant to remove it, but the severe symptoms I was having outweighed my reluctance.

My husband and I were hoping my life would return to normal after the surgery. However, this thyroid removal surgery was the beginning of the darkest period in my life. I didn't recognize at the time how truly important the first encounter of God's presence at the hospital was and how it foreshadowed and marked the start of a long, twelve-year journey. The walk through the valley of the shadow of death was utterly dark, but even in the darkest of days, I perceived God's presence.

CHAPTER 2

Edge of the Valley

The thyroid surgery was supposed to alleviate all my symptoms since the thyroid itself was removed entirely along with six lymph nodes, but it was to no avail. The physical symptoms came raging back, and others now reared their ugly head. It was like something out of *Star Wars: Episode I*, when Jar Jar Binks, Obi-Won Kenobi, and Qui-Gon Jin were navigating their ship through the deep ocean crevasses of Naboo. Out of nowhere, a giant fish tried to swallow them up. Suddenly, an even larger fish lunged out to eat the smaller fish—and *whammy!* Just when you think you're out of danger, Leviathan lunges, rearing his ugly mug, trying to eat all the fish and your ship! This scenario is how physical ailments showed up in my body: one after the other and each one bigger than the last.

All the follow-up surgery appointments and dealing with the cancer diagnosis put me in the spin cycle of appointments. The specialty physician consultations were also in full swing; two or three doctors' visits were commonplace weekly, plus lab work and any tests that were routinely ordered. All of this happened while I was still employed fulltime with the government. Needless to say, work began to have its challenges. When I would conduct interviews with a headset, while my colleagues in the background were also conducting interviews, I began to notice my hearing was decreasing. I delayed for a while, but finally went in for a hearing test and found that I needed hearing aids in 2009.

In addition to the doctor appointments, physical therapy also began since the muscle spasms and loose joints were a daily battle. I found myself explaining to everyone the "spoon theory." In a nutshell, the spoon theory is a way to conserve energy. You have ten spoons, which is all your energy for one day. Getting up, showering, and getting dressed was five spoons, and if I knew I had an appointment that day, I would often choose not to take a shower in the morning because the amount of energy spent—or "spoons" used—was too high, so I would conserve energy for a later time in the day. Another example is if I knew the kids were coming over, I would save energy for their visit instead of using it on something else. The fatigue from constant pain was the new normal. All the while, working full time was like walking a tightrope: one foot on and one foot falling off in an attempt to keep moving along.

One of the specialists who recommended the thyroid surgery also wrote a referral for a consultation at a research hospital. The thyroid removal did not alleviate all my symptoms; in fact, the new laundry list of things that drained my energy was daunting. So, off I went to the research hospital to see the geneticists. The days of questions, blood tests, physical examinations led to another whammy! The findings were a genetic collagen disorder that causes havoc in your body and produces a variety of unwanted effects, and the doctors informed us there was no known cure. So, again, I was faced with a daunting diagnosis that seemed impossible to live with.

I began questioning everything I was doing. Why now? Why didn't the doctors find this at birth, or even sometime after? Why was it rearing its ugly mug now? This genetic syndrome has varying degrees of severity, and different factors escalate the severity of symptoms. Now, with this diagnosis, a whole new world of devices came into my life. This latest diagnosis baffled me, particularly as someone who did sports as a teen like varsity cross-country, swimming, competitive tennis, triathlons, and skiing.

The research quest continued because the single genetic diagnosis did not explain all my crazy symptoms. The pain was getting intolerable, and life was nowhere near "normal." In searching for answers to health problems, I found myself questioning, researching, and talking to others about what they have experienced.

I had no peace about what was going on in my body at the age of forty-one. I decided to attempt to get my life back to normal as best I could. I started walking again daily; even though the pain was great, I pushed through it. When I thought things were beginning to get better, the second research hospital confirmed the genetic syndrome and stated that I had yet another rare disease and that there was no cure. Ugh! What?! Nothing made sense to me. My eyes were focused on the symptoms and diseases the doctors diagnosed. Every time I focused on the diseases ravaging in my body, peace left me.

The research doctor gave me more referrals for body braces to help alleviate joint pain, dislocating joints, and help prevent falling. So, off I went to get the leg braces, since that seemed like the most reasonable of all options. I had hoped the leg braces would help me walk longer each day so that I could get back into a better state of health. For a while, my sheer determination to get my health back seemed to be working. I lost all the steroid weight from thyroid surgery. Boy, did I sure balloon out during that time. I gained *four* clothing sizes in one year due to all the steroids needed to reduce inflammation and treat the thyroid and multisystem issues that were going on. The weight gain really affected my self-image, and I began withdrawing from family pictures and not allowing photographs of me. Thankfully, the new braces helped me to be able to walk miles every day and lose weight. This new body, back to a much smaller size than I had been in years, was quite a victory. The ankle brace success led to other brace fittings, and after a while, I had an array of full body armor to battle simple, everyday tasks.

A little later, after my initial set of leg braces, I used to joke that I was Iron Man because I had so many braces for various parts of my body to help with stability and pain issues from my collagen syndrome. The grandkids would say, "Be careful, watch out for Grammy's 'poppy' joints." Frequently, I dropped jugs of milk, broke many a glass due to dropping them on the tile floor, and would need my husband's help for the most menial of tasks.

The constant bruising also was a sight to see because there were so many of them, and at times they were enormous. I constantly bumped into things. The doctors call it "proprioception", knowing—or in my case, not knowing—where your body is in space. When navigating around my house or when out and about, I ran into things so hard that either I or the object would fall. Beyond the braces and bruises, the silver-ring splints were quite an eyecatcher as well. Most people who saw the ring splints on my hands thought they were funky rings. The ring splints did help me to not drop things, stop dislocations of fingers, and help with the pain.

All these medical devices opened another can of worms with our finances. It seemed like every time the doctors prescribed something else, the cost kept getting higher and higher. The reality of the pain and an increasing inability to move as I used to had become very alarming. So, my husband was willing to spend money on anything that would help, even it was just a little help. We managed to shift things around, giving up on extras, and my husband worked very hard to provide and make things work.

Then came the IVIG (intravenous immunoglobulin) treatments that began right before my thyroid surgery. They were quite costly, and doctors prescribed them every two weeks.

The initial time of getting this medication was daunting. I walked into a medical office building and stayed from 9:00 am until after regular closing hours because my body was reluctant to receive the new IV medication. The following three days, I was in bed with extreme fatigue. Thereafter, these outpatient infusions appointments lasted for eight to ten hours each visit. Since the initial IV infusion in 2007, my veins did not tolerate the thick medication and length of time to administer. The outpatient appointments spending such long hours in a chair hooked to an IV took a toll on my arms and my body. Those first infusions of immuno-globulin left me tired and not able to get out bed for a few days. Little did I know just how far the human body could go to revolt against medications! I would soon find out. All the medical devices pilling up, new thera-pies, and frequent doctor appointments made me feel like a human guinea pig. Determined to find a cure, I researched constantly.

During my daily work for the government, I dealt with people with disabilities most of the day. After I would get home, I would scour the internet, searching for any information on how to cure what the doctors had newly diagnosed. The searches would take me into the wee morning hours because I did not want to stay in the precarious condition of needing all the medica-tions and therapies and having to spend so much time at medical appointments In all this searching, I had faith that God was God of all, but I took it upon *myself* to find for a cure to all the diseases which were consum-ing me. Yes, my husband and I went to church, prayed, and read our Bibles; we did all the things one does who believes in God. Yet, with all this love and knowledge of God, the seeking for the Lord somehow got trampled over by the seeking for a cure. This seeking in my heart somehow transferred to Google more than the Word of God for answers. Instead of the long hours reading and soaking in the Word, I would be reading new research studies on experimental drugs and even sign up for rare disease studies. This thirst for a cure could not be satisfied. The searches took me onto a crooked path to the edge of the valley of the shadow of death, where every turn seemed to lead me to the same bleak place.

CHAPTER 3

Groundhog Day

The walk through the valley of the shadow of death looked like a deep, dark, and crooked path that repeated itself day in and day out. Oh, the insanity of it all! Each day started to meld together. The appointments, therapies, and blood tests continued day in and day out. Working full-time became quite a challenge. Not only was I getting used to different braces for various body parts, but I learned that, in fact, the pill form of thyroid replacement medication was actually making me sick because it contained gluten. Back in 2003, doctors had finally diagnosed celiac disease after years of stomach pain, so I followed a rigorous gluten-free diet. The only alternative to a pill was to inject 100mg of Synthroid into each shoulder every morning. I found myself in the storeroom before work injecting my medication because it had to be taken early in the morning, and my shift began at 7:00 a.m. after the long drive to work.

The 501 accommodations began to pile up as the diseases were taking a toll on my body. Working for the government was a blessing and yet an arduous task at times. I found myself needing extra help to carry out my daily job duties. I needed an air filter at my station to help reduce the possibility of contracting a disease at work from close contact with people. My job entailed interviewing the public, and the workspace was tight, so to limit my exposure, I had a high-tech air filter at my desk, but it needed clearance before it could be used.

The autoimmune disease the doctor diagnosed was the reason I frequently had infections and was susceptible to things other people were not. I always had sinus, ear, upper respiratory, and bladder infections that required antibiotics. The infections didn't go away quickly; some needed two or more rounds of medications or IV antibiotics. Thus, was the case with pneumonia. After the first time, I basically died during surgery; my lungs became the weakest link, and infections set in there. CVID (combined variable immunodeficiency) was not somethings a civil servant who had daily contact with the public needed to have. Pneumonia reared its head often, and so the air filter at work was a must-have.

Another 501 accommodation was for a headset that would accommodate the hearing aids I needed. The hearing in my left ear was suddenly decreasing, and when your job is speaking to people all day long, good hearing is essential. The audiologist fit me with a new type of hearing aid in both ears. This pair was my second set of hearing aids since 2009. After receiving a new pair, it was very apparent how much I needed them. My husband did not have to blare the TV anymore, I was no longer saying, "What did you say?" to everything that was happening, and I could hear tones I had not heard in quite some time.

The hearing aids greatly improved communication with my family members. My husband and I would help family throughout the years, but my body often revolted and made the simplest of tasks difficult, so my husband actually did more of the helping than me. In fact, my arms just wouldn't do what I wanted them to do. Helping family was very important to Jeff and me, not only because we have five children, but because it's just something we have always done together: help people. The doctor told me that if I continued to stress my body out by doing physical tasks, it would speed up the disease process, which was almost at hyperdrive already. My husband always wanted to lend a hand to any of our children whenever they asked, as did I. It was just our nature to help people, no matter what the cost.

The daily typing load at work put a lot of stress on my hands and arms. Even with arm braces and finger splints, I still needed another 501 accommodation. This one was for Dragon software to help with all the typing. After the accommodation was approved, the installation took some time, as did the scheduling of the program training. My absenteeism was extremely high at his point in time due to various treatments, doctor visits, and unrelenting pain that technical training for the software kept causing. I finally got to complete the Dragon software training, which was designed to help me not type as much throughout the day. I pressed on in spite of all the endless cycles of negative reports from the doctors.

The pain and loss of function in my arms were so terrible that a highly qualified hand specialist's visit was more than warranted. This particular doctor is not only a surgeon, but he has a vast knowledge of the collagen syndrome that was causing so much damage in my body. One consult gave me hope of restored function and reduction of pain.

In March of 2014, I had fourteen surgeries on my left arm to lessen the effects of Ehlers-Danlos syndrome. The operation was to improve strength, reduce pain, and help strengthen the function of my arm. However, once again, whammy! I stopped breathing during this surgery as well. Again, for the second time in my life, doctors had to help me breathe artificially during surgery. My husband sounded the alarm, asking why they were not helping me more as I laid there, pale and motionless.

After the operation, in the recovery room from what was supposed to be a day surgery, the nurses told my husband that I would be ready to go home. He was distressed by the fact that I would not respond to anything. I was slumped over and wasn't breathing well. As my husband recalls, a new nurse came and told him that he would have to wheel me outside across the street to the emergency room. With total unbelief at what was happening, he did just that; he sat me in a wheelchair and wheeled me into the ER. As soon as the ER nurse took my vitals, everything quickly changed. My blood oxygen levels had plummeted into the upper seventy percent range, and most people do not recover from this. Nurses had to continually monitor blood oxygen levels, nerve function, and lung capacity.

I spent ten days in the ICU/telemetry unit, all from an outpatient day surgery! Upon discharge, the doctors explained my left lung had partially collapsed from the operation. This surgery left me in worse shape than when I went in. My body was sluggish to recover, the pain was beyond measure, and things were spiraling out of control.

In the aftermath of this day surgery, I was still employed full time for the government. On a massive scale, the sick days had accrued; I was in the hole, minus sick days from all the leave taken. The ICU stay this time left me far worse, and returning to work seemed impossible. At this point, my doctors decided I could no longer work. They told me to file for disability benefits and that it was my only choice. The arm surgery tipped the scale; my body had not recovered from the surgery, and the disease process was accelerating. The disability application took quite some time to process because I had to file for disability retirement since I was a federal employee. It was very upsetting to leave my job. I found much joy in public service and had put in many years as a civil servant.

At this point, my husband and I didn't do much anymore besides attend church and go to the hospital. Attending church was very important to us and a big part of our married life. However, I was no longer teaching Sunday school, volunteering as a camp counselor, or attending prayer groups. Just getting up and getting ready to go places was exhausting at this point. This was when I started experiencing excruciating waves of pain that shot through my body. My lower back set us on a whole other unknown path.

When my husband and I were driving home from church one Sunday, I started screaming in horrible pain. Not understanding what was going on because I was crying uncontrollably, he pulled over. I somehow managed to get myself out of the car and hunched over, continuing to scream and cry in agony. This episode went on for what seemed to be an hour, but it was only about twenty minutes in reality. This horrid episode of pain drastically changed our trajectory, taking us precariously close to a path of no return.

The days melded together: medication, pain, appointments, more medication, more pain, and more appointments. Church attendance became even more infrequent. The pain was so bad I did not let church friends or even close family members touch me very much. I found it physically painful to hug my children. When this began, my heart sank. I had endured two surgeries that almost took my life and beat cancer, yet I was on a repetitive, crooked path that kept leading me closer to a very undesirable dark place.

Much of the time, the place my husband and I went most was the emergency room. The trips to the ER were frequent, and it felt like being stuck in a washing machine's spin cycle: tossed around and spun silly! I distinctly remember one ER visit where the doctor looked at me and said, "We will do our very best to make sure you make it out of here." That statement shook me to my core. I had no idea things had gotten that bad. I knew I was in severe pain, and I knew things were spiraling out of control since my body literally was falling apart at the seams with dislocated joints, ripped muscles from severe muscle spasms, and veins that would explode for no reason. My veins decided to burst and leave me bruised, so bruised at times it looked like someone beat me. On that ER trip, I left the hospital feeling physically and emotionally weak. The words of the doctor kept racing through my mind, and I felt myself beginning to sink.

So many questions raced through my mind. Why is all this happening? What did I do to have this happen? What was next? Time and time again, as I pondered life, I would find God in the stillness and be reminded that God is bigger than my circumstances. I turned to my Bible instead of Google, focusing once again on God's Word and not focusing on the diseases coursing through my body. My trust was in God, not Google. Peace had come in the midst of the storm. The peace that surpasses all understanding strengthened me to carry on. It gave me the strength to not give up and not give in to the negative reports and finality of what the doctors were saying.

CHAPTER 4

Deep in the Valley of the Shadow of Death

June of 2014 hit like a ton of bricks after I received a letter from my doctor that said I only had a few years to live due to the two fatal diseases the physicians had diagnosed. Never had my husband and I expected this to happen to us. We loved each other deeply, and the idea of not being here on this earth with him broke my heart. In profound sadness, I traversed deep into the valley of the shadow of death.

Stunned by what the doctor said, I was gasping for truth. How could this be? How could my life be ending so soon? Why? The questions kept arising as my husband and I went into survival mode. Just surviving the day became the new normal. Each day had its bumps; some were mountains, and some were rocky mud puddles, but we managed to get through. Jeff remained steadfast in reading the Word every morning, I still had my faith, and we clung to the fact that God is good *all* the time.

This trudge through the valley went on precariously, as the conditions had piled up with two rare, fatal diseases at the top of the list, and spiraling down was a myriad of diseases for which I needed copious amounts of medication to ease. The list of diagnoses included Ehlers-Danlos syndrome, stiff-person syndrome, vasculitis, combined variable immunodeficiency, asthma, GERD, undifferentiated connective tissue disease, IBS, celiac disease, hearing loss, autonomic dysfunction, facet arthropathy, diabetes, and hypoxemia, to name a few.

Treating all the diagnoses required a vat of medication, which I kept by my side all the time. The medication list was lengthy due to the daily, as needed, and emergency medications prescribed by the doctors. The list included twenty-nine medicines by 2015. The sheer number of drugs and the number of pills taken per day required a strict schedule. Managing all the medicines was a full-time job. Daily, I wrote down the name of the medication, time taken, and why I was taking med; if it was as-needed, I wrote down what was causing me to need the prescription. I did this to report back to doctors to help them understand what I was going through each day.

The crooked valley paths just kept taking me places I did not want to go. They took me from a kidney injury, to a thirty-day hospital stay for surgery to put in a stint, to emergency surgery to remove the stint because of abdominal swelling that moved the stint out of place, and other very long hospital stays. It was during that thirty-day hospital stay that doctors decided I needed a port implanted in my chest so I could receive intravenous medications. My veins were bursting at this point in large numbers, and medications were not getting delivered through IV placements in my arms. The result: an implanted chest port, where a tube is placed in your jugular vein and a small, heart-shaped device with a tube out the bottom end goes into your heart. This port was how I would get medications rapidly, and my body seemed to welcome the process since my arms did not want to be pin cushions for all blood tests and IV starts for medications any longer. My body had utterly rejected the intravenous medications through my arms that I had received since 2007.

Before I got my aforementioned chest port, every other Monday, I received immunoglobin therapy, but after a few years, my veins kept bursting and would not allow the thick immunoglobulin IV medication in. So, the next step was a medical device that administered the thick medication in lesser amounts into my stomach tissue. I had to be trained how to take a needle, secure it under the skin on my stomach area, and correctly dispense the medication into myself over a few hours at home instead of in a hospital setting. This method of self-injecting into my stomach went on a few more years until the kidney injury. There was no way to get the medications in me; my stomach had been leaching out the meds and my veins burst anytime an IV tried to be started on my arms. So, the chest port was the only option.

After the thirty-day kidney injury hospitalization, I got out only to go back inpatient with neck swelling, difficulty breathing, and facial swelling. For days on end, doctors tried many different remedies, to no avail. I kept saying, "Something isn't right. Something is not right; please do something." The vast number of medications seemed to be having an adverse effect on me.

I believe it was forty days later when the doctors discharged me—not because they found out what was causing all the unwanted and potentially life-threatening symptoms, but because doctors had no other course of action to take. So, I was discharged and went to my allergist/autoimmune doctor, who ran a few tests and found that I was allergic to Benadryl! The hospital had been giving me Benadryl via IV the whole time during the forty-day stay to reduce swelling and inflammation in my face and neck, but the Benadryl is what caused all that. So, no more Benadryl for me, ever! The simple medications the average person can take with no side effects—my body profoundly rejected. Before taking any medication for the first time, I would have to pre-treat with steroids to not have an allergic reaction. In my medical chart, the allergy list was as long as or longer than the current problem list of medical conditions treated by physicians listed in my medical chart.

If three surgeries back-to-back-to-back were not enough, I then had a sudden profound loss of hearing in my left ear, pain in my neck, imbalances issues, and numbness. Another trip to the doctor: a neurosurgeon, who furnished the news that I needed brain surgery. Brain surgery! Gah! This drastic turn was so uncharted. I found myself bolted to a table under a gamma knife every day for a week. Lucky me, I was one of the one percent of people who can see the gamma knife in their field of view. Every pulse of the gamma-ray I saw cutting into the tumor; or, in more technical terms, the unilateral vestibular schwannoma.

The red light pierced my vision for hours each day. I lay on that tabled bolted down under a metal face mask asking God more questions. *Why? Why me? Where are You in all this?* Learning from the past, I stopped asking, "What more can happen?" I remember not even having any more questions to ask God; laying on that operating table, I knew He could hear me and that He was there even in that horrid place. I was not alone. I thanked God for listening to me rant about all the crap I was going through. I thanked Him for not leaving me even though He felt very far away. I thanked the Lord for His peace and His plan for my life.

After the nurse unbolted me from the surgery table for the last time, I spoke with the neurologist, who reminded me that the surgery was necessary because where the tumor grew on my nerves was right at the base of the inner ear and spine, and if the tumor grew, it would have cut off my spinal cord. I would have become paralyzed from the neck down. The discussion of being paralyzed is why the decision was made to endure brain surgery and all the entanglements that came with it while my body was camped out in the valley of death.

The sheer amount of medications needed to endure laying on the table for the gamma knife procedure was mind-boggling. My port was accessed 24/7 to deliver the necessary medicines rapidly. The large doses of steroids ballooned my body out once again. My self-esteem plummeted the larger I grew and the larger my belly and neck ballooned out. My husband always had the same reply when I would say I looked fat: "You're beautiful." I couldn't receive the compliment, but he always told me he loved me and how beautiful I looked.

To me, my body looked like a marshmallow man: puffy, lumpy, and huge! I could not stand to look in the mirror any longer. I made my husband remove mirrors in our home except for one small one in the upstairs and downstairs bathrooms. When I looked in the mirror, all I saw was sickness. The days were hijacked by relentless pain after the brain surgery, ballooning out from medications, and from the diseases having progressed

Everything started to revolve around pain management because the spasms were increasing exponentially, causing my bones to dislocate, muscles to rip off my bones, and organs to move out of their correct positioning. One hospital stay was so bad due to the spasms that I dislocated my shoulder while in a hospital bed. The doctors wanted to set it back in, but I insisted on doing it myself because other people touching me would just set off the spasms even more. These were not ordinary spasms; they would be like a Charley horse from Hades and last forever. Not knowing when or why they came on was the worst. I could be just sitting there, watching TV, then scream bloody murder as my muscle tightened and squeezed my body. Valium was what doctors prescribed to help stop the spams. However, the spasms never stopped.

The Valium didn't always help; it was more like a band-aid. However, when the gut-wrenching spasms twisted my muscles to the juncture of them ripping off my bones or squeezing my neck muscles to the point I could no longer breathe, the medicine brought some relief to the madness. The spasms came on from different things that startled me due to the acceleration of the rare autoimmune neurological condition the doctors diagnosed in 2012. This disease runs a fast course, ending in the total incapacitation of one's body. This prospect did not look good as things exponentially accelerated after brain surgery.

2015 was bad enough, and 2016 almost drove the nail all the way in to seal the coffin. The trudge through the valley of death was so dark that there were only whispers of a glimmer of getting out. There were so many hospitalizations in 2016, more than any other year, but in January of 2017, I dug deep and mustered up the energy to go to the Week of Refreshing conference at church. The speaker that night, a well-known man of God, called people up to pray for them. I did not want to be called out. In fact, I did not even want to be in the meeting anymore and wanted to leave, but I could not find the right moment to leave. I desperately needed a touch from God though.

I had been seeking the Lord for a very long time for healing. I prayed, read the Word, and asked people to pray for me for year after year. In the past years of attending the Week of Refreshing conference, I received prayer and asked many people to pray for healing. This time, however, something seemed off. I ended up standing in front of the man of God, who proceeded to pray for me. He grabbed my hands, and I began to cry. I was crying from sheer pain, not crying under the power of God. I did not know how to get out of the precarious situation. I listened to the words he spoke and prayed, but I could not really hear anything but my body screaming in pain at me. I left that night bawling in pain and confusion at what transpired. I knew God spoke through people. I have witnessed Him move mightily so many times for so many years, but I left church disappointed and not healed, once again.

The questions flurried: *Why not me, Lord? Why am I not healed? Why did others walk out free from pain and sickness and not me? Please help me understand. Help me, Lord. Why did I even go? Well, it hit me: did I go to church for Him, or did I go just to get something?* I pondered much as I had to take even more medication to ease the pain in my hands. That night stayed with me for a very long time. I continued to ponder the questions in my heart: why did I go the church that night? What was the condition of my heart?

In March of 2017, there were more hospitalizations with surgery, to no avail. The valley became very bleak at every turn. The negative words were piling in from every side. By June of 2017, things came to the breaking point. I went yet again for more surgery for another port. Another port needed to be switched out for a new one. Yet again, the medications administered sent me into respiratory failure. It was like we were in a never-ending spin cycle of bad reports and surgeries that went wrong. Jeff found himself desperate after hearing the doctors report how low my oxygen levels were and that I was barely breathing. There was a full code during surgery, they admitted once again.

Jeff called people to ask for prayer. The prognosis the doctors gave him was grim. They told Jeff I would not regain my mental abilities due to an extended period of low oxygen. For ten days, Jeff sat with me as I lay in the hospital bed. I do not recall any of this hospital stay. I have no recollection of being in the hospital except for tiny flashes of Jeff's face, and I have a speck of memory of Pastor Keith Kippen being in the hospital room.

My husband says Pastor Keith Kippen and I had a very long discussion about hell. I have zero memory of it. Jeff had called Pastor Keith because Jeff was beside himself. Jeff was in shock and needed help. Fortunately, Pastor Keith had already been at the hospital visiting someone when he received Jeff's call. He came right away to my hospital room. Jeff was very thankful for the visit, prayer, and encouragement from Pastor Keith.

I still am baffled as to why I have no memory of the visit with Pastor Keith and the long discussion about dreams we both had about going to hell. I do not remember the conversation or the entire hospital stay for that matter. The last day, Jeff says the doctors were at their wits' end too, so it was an abrupt end to the stay, and he drove me to another hospital. I have my first concrete memory from waking up after the surgery but in another hospital. After some brief medical treatment, we went home that night to get some much-needed rest.

The next morning, I asked Jeff to take me to church. He was exhausted and disbelieving of how I had any energy to go to church. I knew in my being that I needed to go. My loving husband obliged despite his fatigue and watched over me at church. I took my purple prayer covering, kneeled on the altar at church, and just soaked in God's presence.

I know God hears every word and every cry; in fact, God knows of every single tear. However, I had no more tears and no more words that day. I had nothing to say but to position my heart before the Lord. I vaguely remember someone coming and gently laying their hand on my shoulder, but I was in a different place. After some time, I looked back at Jeff, and he helped me up, and we went home. We made it through worship, but not the message. It was no matter; the Lord knew why I went: to encounter His presence. Whatever it was that the Lord deposited in me helped me to endure the next dark crevasse on the dark path. Yet again, the Lord did not leave nor forsake me. The Lord was with me on the journey through the valley of the shadow of death.

The news the next day came: *whammy!* It was like a ton of bricks had fallen down on us, pushing us farther into the dark crevice in the shadow of death: homecare! Homecare seemed like it was for someone who was in a bad state, unable to do anything for themselves, and needed constant care. Wait. How could that be for me? Was I really at that place? I found myself having nurses and physical therapists come to my home a few times a week. They inspected our house to make sure it was a safe place to be, and of course, it was very safe, thanks to my husband. Weeks, then months went by, and I spent more time sleeping, not getting up much, nor eating a lot. The physical therapist stopped coming, and then the nurses said we had the medications under control, and we could do the wellness check virtually or by phone. We had 24/7 access to nurses and a doctor.

Fall of 2017 rolled in with more surgery. I'd had enough: enough of the hospital, enough medications, and enough time spent at doctors' offices. The end of the valley seemed like it had to be around the corner. The homecare stopped, and we rarely made it to the church at this point. Things looked so bleak that I remember saying to my husband that if we can just make it to church, something good will come if we try. So, we tried, and we made it. Pastor Keith Kippen preached that Sunday, and all I remember is him prophesying, "2018. 2018 is going to be the best year of your life." I grabbed onto those words in my heart. I heard Pastor Keith say it a few times, and each time, it rang out deeper in me. I thought, *Why not? Why couldn't 2018 be the best year of my life?*

On the way home, I told my husband, "2018 is going to be the best year yet." He turned and smiled at me. We were so thankful to have made the trip to and from the church without any massive rapid decline in my health, as any outings usually caused my body to swirl down into meltdown mode. Thankful for the prophetic word of the Lord that 2018 would be the best year of my life, and I believed. We believed. My husband always stood by me, especially when it came to hearing from the Lord. I knew in my heart that the words declared were for me.

CHAPTER 5

Selfless

Through all the mayhem, the one constant in my life was my husband, Jeff. This man worked tirelessly, sacrificing himself for me. He was always there; daily, he laid down his life for me. He attended to everything I needed and so much more. Jeff did things for me that I never thought I would need a husband to do. Being self-employed enabled him to care for me, drive me to the endless doctor appointments, stay by my bedside at the hospital, take care of our home, and manage to help the kids with what they needed as well. He did all that on top of caring for the farm animals, who needed to be fed and watered twice a day. This man worked more hours in one day than humanly imaginable for years!

Every day, Jeff would get up, read his Bible, and drink his coffee. He has always read the Bible cover-to-cover and then started all over again. At the beginning of our marriage, I had no idea how valuable the time Jeff spent every morning reading his Bible would be to our family. This time was well-spent because he drew upon the strength of the Word to help carry me through the valley. On the days that I had no strength, when I'd be screaming and crying out in agony, saying, "I can't do this anymore," he would gently speak over me: "Yes, yes, we can do this. We will get through this." His genuine love for me and tender heart shined through every selfless act he carried out. Yes, I say an act of love, because no man eagerly desires to help their wife go to the bathroom, shop for feminine products, clean toilets, get dressed, pick up mess after mess from medications, and clean spilled food or water messes because I couldn't grip things properly. Jeff never complained, he just *did*. He took care of everything I possibly needed and more.

One hospital stay, I hadn't eaten because there was no gluten-free food available at the hospital. The lack of food options often happened because hospitals offered a gluten-free alternative, but not *certified* free of gluten. That means that there is still a small amount of gluten in non-certified gluten-free products, so I couldn't eat any of the hospital food because I would get very sick and it would cause a domino effect in my autoimmune system. Jeff had even transformed our home into a gluten-free zone with a dedicated fridge and stove for no cross-contamination of foods containing gluten. So, the trek home from the hospital to make me food was Jeff's solution to this problem.

My husband would go home every morning, feed the animals, and return with a scrambled egg sandwich on gluten-free bread and a bottle of Smart Water. Then, when I slept during the day at the hospital, he would leave and go to the store next to the hospital and buy gluten-free crackers, cheese, and lean meat for me to eat. Attempting to make the lengthy hospital stays more tolerable, Jeff also brought my books from home and clean clothes so that I could feel at least half-human. He was always thinking about me and how he could help me get better. His love of the Word served as his anchor. I am sure there were times he was overwhelmed, scared, tired, or angry, but I didn't see any of that. I observed and felt his love; my husband's love covered me.

I witnessed 1 Corinthians 13 (a passage on love in the Bible) radiate from my husband at every turn through his kindness, humility, and love. Jeff never gave up on me, on us, nor on the goodness of God; even through all the heartache of negative doctor reports, his love for me never failed. Repeatedly, while in the hospital, the nurses told me that my husband would leave me. Yup, time after time, the nurses would administer the medications and then give me the "talk." They said that most husbands leave their wives in "these circumstances," so it was better to prepare myself for the "inevitable." Upon my husband returning to the room, I would tell him what the nurses said, and he was aghast. When this occurred, he became even more vigilant at my bedside. We also had many occurrences of wrong medications administered through my port, which caused serious complications and added undue pain and sickness for me. Jeff sat there like a watchdog, continually asking what the nurses were about to administer to prevent further unnecessary complications.

Jeff became well-versed in knowing what to ask the nurses, such as why medications were being given and how much to administer. My husband gained this knowledge early on in our journey through countless hours spent at my side. During the outpatient visits to receive therapy drugs, which lasted eight to twelve hours for one infusion, Jeff focused on the entire process and asked questions about why something was being done. He is a builder by trade, so his "eagle eyes" observe things and then see how they can be improved. The reason he needed eagle eyes is that we are all human, and humans can make mistakes. He would catch the mistakes before they were catastrophic, and I was so very thankful for my husband's keen, watchful eyes.

Even when he was there all the time, some things managed to go south once in a while. During a particular outpatient hospital stay, a nurse skipped one step during the long immunoglobulin infusion process As a result, I bloated out with twenty plus pounds and ended up inpatient for almost a month as they worked to rid my body of excess fluid. I could have gotten mad at the nurse for that mistake, but what would that do? Grace is powerful. If I would have wallowed in the error and let everybody and their mother know about it, well, the atmosphere in my hospital room would have been one of fear. No nurse would want to come in with me if I had repeatedly been reminding them of another's mistake. I am so thankful to my husband for staying at my bedside, encouraging me, and watching over me.

Time continued to go on, but we never seemed to go anywhere but further into the darkness of the valley. However, my husband remained steadfast. A certain night is forever etched in my mind because of the monumental amount of patience and kindness my husband poured out. After getting out of the hospital, I had been sleeping downstairs on our couch because I didn't want to tackle the dreaded stairs. Yet, my husband gently said, "You would be more comfortable up in the bed." The stairs in our house are immensely steep to go from the main floor to the upstairs. The 1912 farmhouse stairs are still intact and have an a very steep incline to the upper rooms in our home. I hunched over the bottom step, looked up at the daunting task as I cried out in pain from muscle spasms, and said, "I can't do this. Lord, help me." I put all my effort into pulling my foot onto the next step, grabbed the rail with both arms, and then attempted to pull myself up to the second step, but stopped immediately as muscle spasms began ripping my lower back and leg muscles. Jeff patiently assisted me saying, "We will get upstairs, one step at a time. We've got this. Almost there. I am here." These are the words he spoke over and over as I screamed in excruciating pain.

We finally made it up the stairs after what seemed like half an hour of me screaming bloody murder as he spoke encouraging words and offered any assistance I could tolerate. Once in bed, I laid in my survival position. I often stayed in this position for hours a day; Jeff referred to it as "cocooning." I wouldn't move a muscle; I would allow no noise in the room nor motion of any kind to try and prevent muscle spasms from coming on in the hopes of bringing a fraction of relief to the pain surging through my body. The days of me going up and down the stairs with ease were long-gone, and Jeff had to help me now more than ever. I witnessed what long-suffering looks like, watching my husband care for me day in and day out.

He not only endlessly assisted me, but he also showed up for family whenever someone needed help. Before my body was riddled with disease, my husband always used his God-given talents to help family, friends, and anyone who asked. Whether it was building something, fixing vehicles, working on houses, he served other's needs. Even in the valley, he found time to lend a hand to others. These acts of service and genuine kindness inspired me. Our children, especially, were the beneficiaries of my husband's talents. He helped with projects, encouraged them, lent a hand with their own homes, facilitated family events, and also stepped up to fill the holes that the disease in my body left in our family. Jeff's genuineness overflowed and helped keep the peace while weathering the storms in the valley of the shadow of death.

Our children did not know the finality of the doctors' predictions of the fatal diseases they had diagnosed. We thought not telling them of the doctor's letter that I had a few years to live was for the best. We wanted our adult children to live out their own lives without hesitation. By this point, our youngest, Cody, was twenty-five years old, newly married, and had children. Cody and his wife Halley would bring their girls to the hospital to visit. These visits were bittersweet because I got to see Cody and Haley's girls, but I couldn't do much more than look at them and talk to them with all the tubes attached to my body. I am so grateful to them for bringing the little girls to visit; they would bring so much hope and life and would increase my desire to get better.

All our adult children had their own lives to live, and my husband and I encouraged them to do whatever they had a desire to do. Jeff did not want to burden our children with what we were going through, but it was the elephant in the room at every holiday or family gathering. No one knew how I would be or if I would stay for the course of the family event. I didn't even know how I would be or what would happen because each day was varied with pain, weakness, spasms, nausea, horrid stomach issues, loss of vision, and so many more ghastly symptoms, one piled on top of the other. I was wearing an oxygen tube most of the time by this point, and I know it was hard for kids to see me in pain and in such a state. I felt utterly helpless and would rely so much on Jeff during family gatherings, and most all the time, I leaned on him; not just physically to help me get up and down off the couch or the stairs, but emotionally and spiritually. He continued to suffer for me to bear all things that came our way; his love never failed!

This chapter of love from the Bible, 1 Corinthians 13, came to life while we walked through the valley of the shadow of death. Even in the midst of the fierce storms trying to pound us down and force us to give up, love never failed: love covered. My husband's love for the Lord and for me endured. My love for the Lord and my husband fueled me to believe all things. Jeff and I had deep-rooted faith that *God's love does not fail*. The words in the Bible actually came to life for me in watching my husband care for me every single day. These verses on love are incredibly inspiring and filled me with strength in times when I didn't think I could go on another second.

The dreaded ER visits demonstrated just how much love and faith was flowing through my husband. Once again, I was in the emergency room. This time, there was a bit more of a frenzy and serious tone with the ER staff. I remember lying on the bed waiting for the emergency room doctor to come in, and suddenly, the entire left side of my face went numb, and I tried to tell Jeff. I couldn't get my words out, and then the left side of my body went numb. Jeff started yelling for the doctor as the curtain flung open. The doctor took one look at me and yelled out to his staff! I locked my eyes on Jeff as the team of people wheeled me out of the room in the ER. Jeff was then met in that room by a chaplain. The doctors had sent a chaplain in for my husband! My husband kindly greeted the chaplain and said, "Thank you, but there is no need for you to be here; my wife will be just fine." The chaplain politely replied, "Okay, I am around if you need me."

After I woke up in a new room, not knowing how much time had passed, my husband informed me the doctor had code-stroked me and told me about the chaplain. We spoke about the chaplain coming in and how that made him feel. I really think it's harder for the loved ones watching someone go through health challenges than the person battling the disease. I had tremendous guilt over Jeff having to watch me in pain, continuously care for me, and watch over me, especially while I was in the hospital. Yet even when looking with his eyes and seeing all the pain and sickness, his love endured. I believe Jeff's declaration of faith to the chaplain that I was going to be just fine had an enormous effect on the outcome that evening.

1 Corinthians 13:4-8 (NKJV) says, "Love suffers long and is kind; loves does not envy; love does not parade itself, is not puffed up; does not behave rudely, does not seek its own, is not provoked, thinks no evil; does not rejoice in iniquity, but rejoices in the truth; bears all things, believes all things, hopes all things, endures all things. Love never fails." Jeff stood in the gap for me in love and faith, even though at that moment, things looked impossible. We came out on the other side of this ER visit and were discharged home.

I realized what a tremendous gift God had given me during this extremely dark time: my husband. My husband's love for me was more love than I had for myself. All the kindness and love flowing out of him stemmed from his faith in and love for Jesus. Once more, the Word of God was coming to life as I watched my husband lay down his life, and serve me selflessly.

CHAPTER 6

Photos and Medical Records from the Valley of the Shadow of Death

Below is a list of my diagnoses and problems from my medical chart taken from the Swedish Hospital medical record:

Abnormal echocardiogram
Abnormality of uterine cervix
Acoustic neuroma
Acute respiratory failure with hypoxia
Addison's disease
Acute kidney injury
Allergic reaction caused by medications
Asthma

Asthma with asthmaticus

Cardiomegaly

Celiac disease

Cervicalgia

Chest pain

Chronic migraine

Cluster headache

Common variable immunodeficiency (CVID)

Disorder of the autonomic nervous system

Dyspnea (labored breathing)

Ehlers-Danlos syndrome

Eustachian tube dysfunction

Facet arthropathy

Fluid retention

Gastroesophageal reflux disease

Generalized edema

Glucocorticoid deficiency

Hashimoto's thyroiditis

Headache

Hearing loss (both ears)

Heading loss (conductive bilateral)

History of Raynaud's syndrome

History of splenomegaly

Hyperglycemia

Hypermobility syndrome

Hypokalemia (potassium deficiency)

Hyponatremia (low blood sodium)

Hypothyroidism

Hypoxemia (deficient oxygen)

Immunoglobulin deficiency

Intolerance to cold

Iron deficiency

Irritable bowel syndrome

Left lower lobe pneumonia

Left side cerebellopontine syndrome

Left sensorineural hearing loss

Lymphopenia

Malignant neoplasm of thyroid (cancer)

Migraine variant

Nephrolithiasis (kidney stones)

Neurilemmoma (brain tumor)

Orbital inflammatory syndrome

Papillary carcinoma of thyroid

Pelvic mass

POTS (Tachycardia syndrome)

Raynaud's Disease

Scoliosis

Stiff-person syndrome

Trigeminal neuralgia

Unspecified diabetes

Undifferentiated connective tissue disease

Vasculitis

Vitreitis (eye inflammation)

Vocal cord dysfunction

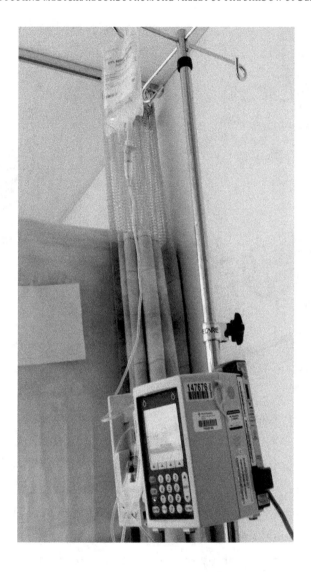

Infusion pole in the hospital, used for administering intravenous medications for hours, days, and years. Being tethered to this pole so frequently made me feel like it was a permanent attachment.

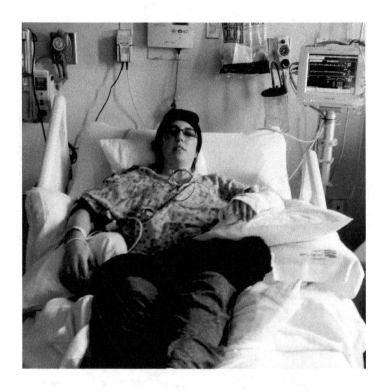

March 14, 2014. Twelve arm surgeries in one day led to a two-week inpatient stay. I landed in the ICU due to having stopped breathing during surgery and having severely low oxygen levels. This led to long-term lung damage. My left lung had partially deflated, collapsed, and would not function properly. This surgery marked the beginning of my severe breathing troubles.

This picture really illustrates how nuts my life was at this point. Doctors kept adding more and more medications for daily use, once a month, as needed, and for use in an emergency. There were so many medications that I had these boxes by my bedside to get through the month.

June 2016, another lengthy hospitalization with no good outcome. The inpatient hospital stays would be twenty to forty days. A few times, I got discharged only to wind up in ER inpatient again soon after.

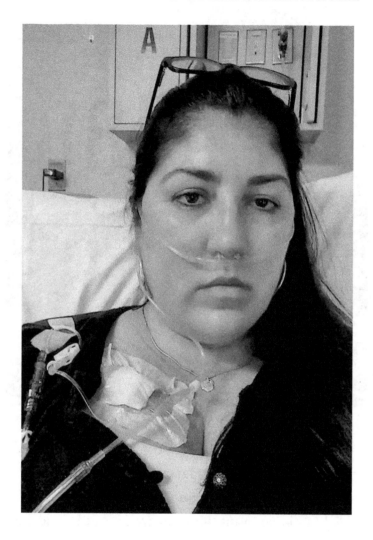

February 2016. I was miserable! This picture doesn't even look like me. It looks like someone sucked all the life out of me. Even more intravenous medications were being given through my port to try to calm down the current storm, to no avail.

When picking these license plates up, I realized that the doctors had "permanently disabled" me. I even had a wallet card designating me as "permanently disabled." I did not want this designation, but I could not walk to my car—even with the help of oxygen—without being short of breath. Walking from our vehicle to the hospital entrance was a whole other can of worms that I dreaded. My body was failing, and the days became very tough to endure.

3901 Hoyt Avenue ▪ Everett, WA 98201 ▪ 425-259-0966

Lisa J Lancaster
Po Box 2544
Stanwood WA 98292-2544

Advanced Imaging
Allergy, Asthma &
Immunology
Anesthesiology
Behavioral Health
Cancer/Oncology
Cosmetic Surgery
Critical Care
Dermatology
Diabetes/
Endocrinology
Ear, Nose & Throat
Family Medicine
Gastroenterology
Geriatric Care
Gynecology
Hand Center
Head & Neck
Surgery
Heart & Vascular
Center
Hearing Aid Center
Hematology
Infectious Medicine
Internal Medicine
Laboratory Services
Neurology
Nephrology
Obstetrics
Occ Medicine
Ophthalmology
Orthopedics
Outpatient Surgery
Centers
Pediatric/Adolescent
Care
Pharmacy Services
Physical Medicine &
Rehab
Physical Therapy
Podiatry
Pulmonary
Rheumatology &
Arthritis
Skin Surgery & Laser
Sleep Center
Spine Center
Sports Medicine
Surgery
Urology
Vision Centers
Walk-In Clinics
Women's Wellness

6/11/2014

Lisa J Lancaster was seen at The Everett Clinic on 06.11.14 for
continued evaluation of her multiple medical conditions.

Ms Lancaster has 2 ultimately fatal diseases for which there is no
known cure.

Her most dangerous active illness is Stiff Person Syndrome (ICD9
code is 333.91) for which there is no cure. and it will progressively
worsen until she is totally incapacitated.

Her second rapidly progressive illness that is also untreatable and
ultimately fatal is her Ehlers Danlos Syndrome Type 3 (ICD 756.83).

Both of these diseases have no viable long term treatment options
and both will prove ultimately fatal in the next few years.

Sincerely,

Paul T Mcbride, MD
Allergy, Asthma and Immunology
The Everett Clinic

Doctor's letter that said I had a few years to live.

57

The Everett Clinic
For the whole you.
3901 Hoyt Avenue ■ Everett, WA 98201 ■ 425-259-0966

Advanced Imaging
Allergy, Asthma &
Immunology
Anesthesiology
Behavioral Health
Cancer/Oncology
Cosmetic Surgery
Critical Care
Dermatology
Diabetes/
Endocrinology
Ear, Nose & Throat
Family Medicine
Gastroenterology
Geriatric Care
Gynecology
Hand Center
Head & Neck
Surgery
Heart & Vascular
Center
Hearing Aid Center
Hematology
Infectious Medicine
Internal Medicine
Laboratory Services
Neurology
Nephrology
Obstetrics
Occ Medicine
Ophthalmology
Orthopedics
Outpatient Surgery
Centers
Pediatric/Adolescent
Care
Pharmacy Services
Physical Medicine &
Rehab
Physical Therapy
Podiatry
Pulmonary
Rheumatology &
Arthritis
Skin Surgery & Laser
Sleep Center
Spine Center
Sports Medicine
Surgery
Urology
Vision Centers
Walk-In Clinics
Women's Wellness

4/28/2014

To Whom It May Concern:

Lisa has been under my care for the following multiple diagnoses:

Immunoglobulin deficiency (279.03), Vasculitis-Primary (447.6),
Hypoxemia (799.02), Ehlers-Danlos syndrome, type 3 (756.83),
Undifferentiated connective tissue disease (710.9), Hashimoto's
thyroiditis (245.2), Stiff person syndrome (333.91), GERD (530.81),
Cough variant asthma (493.82), Ceciliac disease (579.0), Irritable
Bowel syndrome (564.1), Cervicalgia (723.1), Facet Arthropathy
(721.90), Conductive Bilateral Hearing Loss (389.06), Autonomic
Dysfunction Syndrome-Adrenergic , and Allergic Urticaria (708.0).

Many of these conditions are either minimally controlled or not
controlled well at all despite our extensive efforts.

Lisa needs to accept that medical disability is her only option at this
point in time.

If you have any questions, please do not hesitate to contact me.

Sincerely,

Emily Savage, MD
MAIN INTERNAL MED
Department Phone: 425-339-5420

Physician's letter stating that disabilty was the only option.

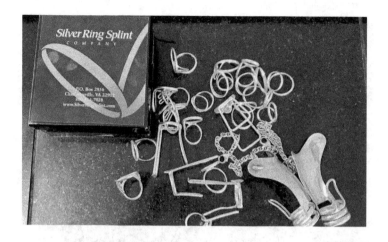

Finger splints, not something I was aware of prior to the many episodes of dropping things, fingers dislocating and subluxing, and pain. Many people who saw these splints on my hands thought they were rings, but in fact, they helped strengthen my joints an allowed me to pick things up without dislocating joints.

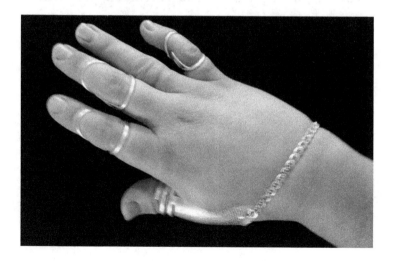

Custom braces for pretty much every joint in my body. I needed varying degrees of support so I had many braces to go back and forth between. Some days, I couldn't move at all; so, I had extreme support to help me walk. Subluxing, dislocating, and extremely painful joints were challenging and exhausting.

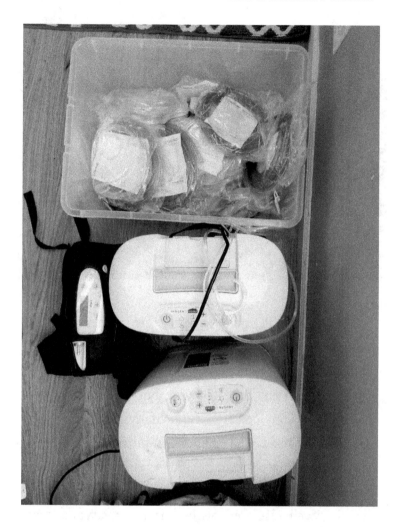

My lungs continued to struggle to function, so I was prescribed oxygen to cope. I had a backpack that went everywhere with me because my oxygen levels would severely drop and stay below acceptable levels. The home oxygen concentrators allowed me to be upstairs and downstairs in my home.

This picture is one of the very few images taken of me during the darkest time of my life. I never wanted my photograph taken by anyone. Saying "no" to all pictures was not the best decision, but I didn't care because I could not look at pictures of myself. When I saw pictures, all I saw was sickness and disease. The decision to not allow photos affected my kids; there are very few photos of me during the time in the valley. I did not do "sick" well. I isolated, pushed friends away, and even took mirrors out of rooms because I didn't want to look at myself and see the sickness. Sickness was not "me." The no photo-taking lasted for years and years.

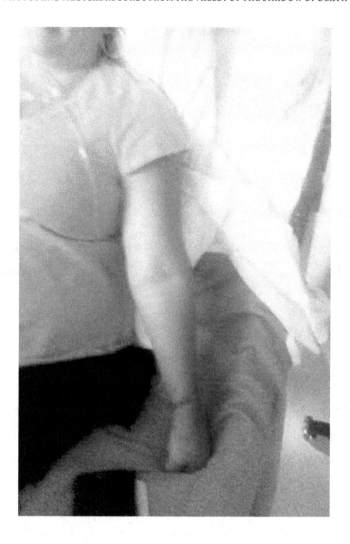

This is the only picture of me at the hospital in the middle of an attack. My muscles would tense up so bad it was like your whole body having an excruciating Charley horse that would never let up. It was hours and hours of agony.

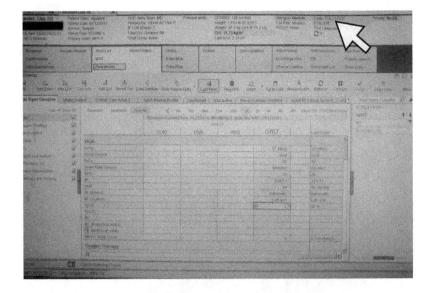

This picture is a screenshot of the hospital monitor in my room. It says "full code" 07/17/2017. Three times in my life, I have experienced a full code in the ER or surgery. This particular full code in July was a very trying time for Jeff because I do not remember any of the inpatient stay after the doctors coded me during surgery to remove and replace my second chest port. The doctors told my husband I would not recover my mental abilities from the prolonged lack of oxygen from having stopped breathing. My husband told me how he would nudge me over and over to coax me to take a breath.

CHAPTER 7

Crying Out: Only Believe

Survival: this was now the state of our position in the valley of the shadow of death. No longer did time pass day by day, but actually, we were trudging each curve moment to moment through the valley trying to navigate our way. The hospitalizations ceased and I was placed on homecare with a nurse and physical therapist. Here I was, a mother of five, not even fifty years old, yet I was on homecare. After the doctors kept saying there was nothing more they could do, the physical therapy stopped, and the vast amount of appointments ended. The medications were there to keep things as the doctors referred to as "tolerable," but there was no comfort in any of it! I had sunk deep in the muck of the valley at this point.

By December of 2017, there was no hope from the medical community of anything changing for the better. We were isolated from our church family of our own doing because we didn't want to burden anyone with the living torment that was ensnaring us. Jeff had to go back to work since the numerous lengthy hospitalizations lead to depleting much our savings account. He never wanted to leave to go to work, but I insisted. Not only did he need to work to pay our bills, but he also needed a break from all the trauma of watching me struggle with pain, spasms, and breathing day in and day out. I wasn't getting out of bed at all except to use the bathroom. I needed oxygen twenty-four seven and didn't eat much anymore. Each moment, life seemed to be fading. I laid in bed, reliving my life over and over in my mind, tears flooding my eyes, asking God, "Why? Why now? Why all the pain and sickness all these years?"

In the middle of me asking God these questions, Jeff came into the room to say goodbye. I couldn't speak much at this point because I had so little energy. He made sure my oxygen was on and told me he was going to work but would be back in just a couple of hours to check on me (I had means to contact help if an emergency arose). Jeff and I locked eyes, and he knew I was telling him, "I love you," without actually saying it. We had a whole conversation with just our eyes. Time seemed to stand still; we stayed in that moment, looking deeply into each other's eyes, not knowing if I would be alive when he got home. Love completely filled the room. I nodded at my husband to leave. Jeff closed the door, and I heard him walk down the stairs and out the front door, then the front door locked. As soon as I heard the front door bolt shut, I burst into tears. I bawled and bawled and didn't have the strength to wipe the tears away from my face.

Laying on my back, I stared up and began to cry out to the Lord. With my whole being, I *cried out to Jesus!* I said, "If You want me here, do something! It's up to You, take me now or do *something!*" In this moment, I completely surrendered I knew deep within me that the Lord heard my cry. Just like in the Word, it says that He hears us when we cry out! Psalm 27:7 (NKJV) says, "Hear, O Lord when I cry with my voice! Have mercy also upon me, and answer me." Psalm 18:6 (NKJV) says, "In my distress I called upon the Lord, And cried out to my God; He heard my voice from His temple, And my cry came before Him, even to His ears." This moment was a total surrender (not ninety-nine percent; a *full* one hundred percent surrender) of body, mind, soul, and strength. I waited in faith upon the Lord. I fully expected Him to do something! I knew the Lord heard the cry from my heart. Whatever happened, I knew it was the Lord's will because I had *no control*, only God did. So, I waited. I waited upon the Lord, my eyes and heart fixed upon Him as I laid in my bed.

I then perceived an overwhelming sense of peace. Love came over me like a warm blanket enveloping me, and the presence filled my bedroom. Suddenly, I had the feeling like I was gliding along underwater effortlessly, absolutely at peace, quiet, and bliss, and for the first time in years, a hope-filled me that surpassed all understanding. As this hope flooded my spirit, I heard the words, "Take the doctor's letter and put it on the altar." I knew exactly what the Lord was asking me to do! He wanted me to take the letter that said I had a few years to live to church and put it on the altar. In my heart, I knew I would obey what the Lord was asking me to do. My faith bubbled up within me.

As I pondered the possibilities of what God was doing, I found I had the strength to get up out of my bed and take a shower. Now, this was no small feat; for years, Jeff had been helping me to get in and out of the shower and sometimes even helped me shower because I had fallen many, many times and hurt myself badly. I stood there under the water and marveled at the fact I was showering, showering without need of oxygen. Afterward, even getting myself dressed was *not* an arduous task that left me breathless. In awe of what was happening, I couldn't wait for Jeff to get home. When he left for work, the thought crossed both our minds that I may not be alive when he returned home.

Waiting for my husband, I sat there, showered, dressed, and full of hope. Jeff walked through the door, and the look on his face was everything! He asked what happened and I told him how I cried out to the Lord with my whole being and then heard Him say to take the letter and put it on the church's altar. So now, instead of planning doctor's appointments, we set a plan to attend church. However, the very next day, I plummeted off a cliff once more into a bottomless pit in the valley. Sickness crept in again all over my body, and I could barely move. My mind battled between what I knew the Lord did in my spirit the day before when He filled me with His strength, His life, His peace, and His love, but then there was the knowledge of what the doctors had said was causing sickness and pain in my body.

The battle to stay focused, my eyes fixed on Jesus, was a moment-by-moment decision. Was I to look to Google as to why things could have plummeted, or was I to choose what I knew in my heart to be true, and fully believe in the Word of God and stand on His promises? I knew I had to obey what the Lord had told me to do, no matter what! For two weeks, I wrestled through the negative words spoken over me for years. I could hear the whispers of doubt and fear trying to override what I knew I was supposed to do, trying to get me not to obey. The doubt was pulling at me, trying to take over my mind and keep me on my sickbed, but God had strengthened me in that beautiful moment of peace, love, and hope. The Lord strengthened me to carry out obedience to the words He spoke and showed me: "It is possible: only believe."

The battle in my mind fiercely raged on for two weeks, but my heart stayed the course. The day came, we packed up my oxygen and medications, and Jeff helped me get dressed. The drive to church seemed longer than usual, but we arrived on a Sunday evening the first night of a conference called the Week of Refreshing at our Church in January of 2018. Walking in, Jeff made sure no one patted me on the back or tried to hug me; he kept a buffer zone around me so no one would unknowingly cause pain by touching me. We listened to the entire message after the worship music. I waited for the right time to take the letter up to the altar. After Pastor Keith finished speaking, I made my way up to the altar, doctor's letter in hand. As I walked closer to the altar, I observed that there was nowhere to place the letter, no receptacle. Pastor Keith happened to be up front on the altar still, I walked right up to him, placed the letter in his hand, and said, "This is not mine." He smiled, looked at the letter, and then prayed for us.

I walked out of the church that night so filled with hope, so full of thanksgiving and praise, so very thankful that I had been obedient to what the Lord asked me to do. I knew in my heart when I handed that letter over and said, "This is not mine," something shifted; something happened, and hope bubbled up even more. Jeff and I both were so thankful to have worshipped, heard a full message, and experienced a complete church service together with no episodes of pain or spasms.

We went home, had dinner, and went to bed very, very thankful. My husband even marveled as I slept that evening. He watched me sleep, not out of fear but out of amazement. I wasn't writhing in pain, moaning, or constantly rubbing my legs as I slept. I didn't wake up and ask him to get pain pills or put the oxygen on. There were no muscle spasms all night. The oxygen wasn't even on me, and I slept that entire night peacefully as my husband marveled.

CHAPTER 8

Out of the Valley: Living Possible

From the moment I woke up after having gone to church to put the letter on the altar, I was pain-free! This act of obedience in doing the very thing God spoke to my heart was a preeminent key to unlocking the pain from my body. My first thought upon waking up pain-free was, *I want to go to church!* The Week of Refreshing conference had just begun, so why not go? I quickly got dressed, fed the dogs, grabbed the car keys, and got in the car, but I had forgotten my journal. I went back inside and ran up the stairs! I stopped at the top, marveling at the fact that I ran, I actually ran up the stairs. Praise God! What a miracle!

I couldn't wait to get to church; the excitement pulsed through my veins. The drive to church was absolutely amazing; the presence of God accompanied me. From a medical standpoint, the drive was uneventful: no spams, no pain; I had forgotten to take my medicine before I left. More astounding, I attended that whole morning conference session with no oxygen. The back-pack with my oxygen concentrator was at home. In awe of all the Lord's goodness, the joy inside bubbled up immensely. The miracles were popping up like popcorn.

I had experienced four miracles in less than twenty-four hours: I was pain-free, running up my stairs, not needing to wear an oxygen pack, and now driving. I had not driven by myself more than the four miles to the store in over three years. I could not drive due to all the medicine I had to take and the possibility of having spams, so I usually left the driving to my husband.

Jeff called, and I didn't answer my phone while I attended the morning conference session. He got concerned, so he called some people to check on me. I wasn't home, and the car was gone! I finally noticed all his missed calls and connected with him. A bit confused, he listened to me go on and on about being pain-free, driving, and running up our stairs, the same stairs that had been our nemesis for the past twelve years. When Jeff arrived home from work, I wanted to go back to church for the evening conference session, but Jeff couldn't understand how I still had energy from being in the morning church session *and* that I wanted to drive myself at night. However, when I hugged him, he knew something was different. I didn't cringe with pain or wince when we hugged. We went to church again that night, experiencing even more joy and strength. Every day that week, morning and evening, I attended the Week of Refreshing conference, and the miracles kept arising. After all those years in the valley, I was now coming out the other side.

The fact that I could bear-hug Jeff, hug my grandkids, and pick things up without dropping them astounded me. I had not put all the braces on my body, nor finger splints, and I didn't need any emergency medications that entire Week of Refreshing. Each day, I journaled all the goodness of God that transpired. I found myself laughing instead of crying! Laughing in His presence, I remembered these words from Psalm 16:11 (NKJV): "In Your presence is fullness of joy." My kids and grandkids started noticing that something was different. Instead of my life being enveloped in sickness, I had emerged from the valley of the shadow with strength and joy, so much joy!

From the thyroid cancer diagnosis in 2007 until January of 2018, twelve years had elapsed. During that time, so many family members, friends, business colleagues, church family, pastors, and prophets had prayed for my healing. I had gone to church conferences for years, asking people to pray for me. Interestingly, in the early years in the valley, when I attended prayer meetings and prayed for other people's healings, I would experience all the pain leave my body. Once I stopped praying, all the pain returned. Those experiences in prayer fueled my desire to be fully healed since I had tasted what it was like to be entirely at peace, pain-free, and had experienced the power of the Lord's presence. Prayer is key to receiving healing, and for me, all those years of pastors, prophets, and family praying for me fanned the flames of healing until the Lord moved mightily and began to answer all the prayers.

Miracles still sprang up after the Week of Refreshing. I spent my days journaling, reading my Bible, and dove into Smith Wigglesworth's complete collection of teachings. Getting up very early to read the Bible, praying, reading Wigglesworth's sermons, journaling, walking, and praying as I listened to worship music was my new normal. In the morning hours of seeking the Lord, His presence surrounded me, and I wanted to stay and soak in His love, peace, and pure joy that filled the atmosphere. Some days, my husband came home from work, and it was like he had just left—I had spent the whole day enveloped in the joy of the Lord.

My husband distinctly remembered one night during the Week of Refreshing conference when he encountered the Lord's mighty hand at work. On the third evening of the conference, I had attended by myself because Jeff had to work in the morning. After I arrived home very late, I went upstairs and went straight to bed. The next morning, Jeff told me he had leaned over to hug me, but the Lord stopped him. The Lord said, "Do not touch her. I am working here." My husband went on to tell me he could feel an anointing on me all night and didn't want to disturb what the Lord was doing in me. Jeff had been processing the tremendous shift in our life, and his attitude changed quickly after witnessing all that was unfolding in front of him. The Lord continued to strengthen me, and daily, I had a choice to make: how was I going to live that day? I chose His joy and all the possibilities that came with abiding in Jesus. I had fully surrendered and was fully alive in Him.

The doctor's visits had to continue, because when you have been diagnosed with not one, but two incurable diseases, doctors don't really have that "they will get better" notification on their radar. So, the infusion treatments every other Monday had to continue until the Lord intervened again. I had stopped taking the plethora of meds prescribed, but the immunoglobulin therapy infused through my chest port continued. One particular treatment day, I sat in the infusion room on the cancer floor of the hospital, angry. I was mad to be back in the hospital when I knew in all of my being that I had been completely made whole, healed of all disease. My attitude that day stunk! Even though I woke up that morning and chose His joy, by the time I got to the hospital and was hooked up to the IV, I had allowed the hospital atmosphere to influence me. After the large

IV bag of Gammaguard started its journey through my veins, I suddenly heard the Lord's voice: "Are you going to stay mad, or are you going to do something?" Instantly, I grabbed the infusion pole and began walking around the eighth floor of the hospital with my worship music playing in my ear buds. By the third time around the floor, words of knowledge were flying out of my mouth, praise was erupting from my body, and I felt God's presence shift the atmosphere. Pure joy flowed through me as I walked the floor, prayed, and thanked the Lord for all His goodness, mercy, compassion, kindness, and love, all while having unwanted medication administered in my body. His presence completely saturated me and pure joy continuously bubbled out.

One nurse pulled me aside and said, "You look so different. What happened?" I told this nurse how the Lord healed me, took all the pain from my body, and she let out a scream, saying, "Praise Jesus!" This nurse had taken care of me for years when I was an inpatient on that floor. She knew the diagnosis in my charts and then witnessed me walking the halls with joy. She walked around the corner, away from the nurses' station, and asked me to pray for her. The Lord overcame all the negatives in that cancer ward atmosphere that day. The power of His presence changed everything: I was now praying for others again, and my heart leaped with joy! Praise and thanksgiving continued to flow for the next eight hours until that infusion finished. I am so thankful to have encouraged others that day instead of sitting in a chair and emanating a lousy attitude! I chose to *allow* the presence of Jesus to shift the atmosphere instead of succumbing to the gloomy hospital atmosphere on the cancer ward.

Every day when I woke up, I had a choice to make: choose life in Jesus, or choose death. Choose His joy, or just go about my day. The medication through my ports continued and, in fact, brought more challenges than good things. The port plugged, and I had chest pain, so I had to go to the specialist to see what could be done. The x-ray of my veins, heart, and port showed that yes, it was indeed plugged. The next day, I returned to the hospital to go through the procedure to unplug the port. When I walked into the infusion room, the nurse held up an x-ray image and said, "They are prepping you for surgery." Confused, I asked, "Why?" The RN then said she had been on the phone with the surgeon all morning because the x-ray showed that the port catheter went down through my heart instead of just being placed in the upper chamber. She then said, "You should be dead!" My husband immediately blurted out a swear word: "Oh, ****!" I put my hand on Jeff's chest, looked straight into his eyes, and said, "*I will be okay. Everything will be okay.*" I then looked at the RN and said, "Do you have the authority to order an x-ray?" She said,

"Yes." The nurse ordered the x-ray, and I walked out of the room. Jeff and I waited for the elevator, and I commented on the fact that he swore. In twenty-five years, he had never uttered one swear word. Jeff was aghast by the news that the chest port was not only plugged but completely in the wrong position, which could kill me right then and there. I assured him again, and I said, "I will be okay." We got on the elevator, the door shut, and I closed my eyes and said out loud, "Sweet Jesus, we need a miracle about now." As I spoke, I locked eyes with a gentleman who heard my cry to the Lord, and he smiled, nodded his head, and walked out of the elevator. The x-ray took about two minutes, and we went back upstairs. Walking into the infusion room, the RN now had two x-rays in her hands: the one taken the day before and the one just taken. She shook her head in disbelief and said, "Your port is now in the correct position." I knew that another miracle had just taken place. I then requested the nurse to access my port; I told her plainly, "My port will work just fine." She seemed a tad annoyed by my request, but obliged and stuck the needle in my chest. As soon as she pulled back on the needle, there was the blood return. My port worked, with no procedure to unplug it. Another miracle! In the past, I had my port unplugged eight times with TPA, a clot-busting drug that unblocks chest ports. Ports do not unplug on their own, especially after the surgeon had verified it was blocked the day prior—but *God!* Another miracle!

My husband and I joyfully walked out of the infusion suite out on the floor and stood at the elevators. The head nurse looked out at me asked where I was going, because they had scheduled me for surgery. I said, "I am perfectly fine; my port works." The other nurses, who so many times had seen me screaming in pain, swollen, with joints dislocated, muscles ripping off from spasms, and veins bursting for no reason were now witnessing me walking out of the hospital with no medical intervention! The *intervention* that day came from Jesus; speaking the name of Jesus out loud. There is no way my port could have moved from the bottom chamber of my heart to the upper chamber and unplugged with zero medication or surgery. That day, I chose life. I spoke life to my husband when I declared to him that I would be okay even though the word spoken over me was death. I spoke life by asking for the x-ray because I knew that God had already healed me. "Death and life are in the power of the tongue, And those who love it will eat its fruit" (Proverbs 18:21, NKJV). I believed, and I spoke life. *All* things were possible. I began to *live* possible.

CHAPTER 9

Muscle Memory

My husband Jeff was still in the process of knowing that mighty healing had taken place in me. Our lives forever changed that night when I obeyed and took the doctor's letter and placed it on the church's altar. Instead of surviving moment by moment in the sludge of despair, sickness, and disease, our illuminated path became stepping stones from one miracle to another. Sometimes, it seemed like Jeff was still stuck in the valley even though I was out on the other side. He would react to things like muscle memory. The memory of sickness remained etched in the forefront of his brain, so his initial reaction to me doing anything would be him thinking I would get hurt or that I couldn't do something without his help.

After a church meeting, Jeff and I began to walk down the stairs, and Jeff grabbed my arm to help me as we descended the first step. I turned and gently swatted his hand away, saying, "I don't need your help, Jeffrey." Pastor Jeshu was at the top step behind us and said,

"Yeah, Jeffrey, Lisa doesn't need your help anymore." I laughed as I skipped all the way down the stairs. What seemed impossible just a few months earlier was now entirely possible and doing it joyfully. Going down a staircase was no longer a monumental task. In that moment, I realized that Jeff needed to go through his own process of healing the muscle memory from walking through the valley of the shadow of death.

In March of 2018, some Bethel School of Supernatural Ministry students came to our church. Jeff and I went to the evening church meeting, and we thoroughly enjoyed the worship that night. Our entire married life, going into the church and worshipping together has held a special place in our hearts. We know without even saying that standing there before the Lord, thanking Him, and praising Him together fills our love tanks beyond measure. That's why the trials in the valley were such a tremendous struggle; we couldn't do what we loved to do together because I could not stand in church, sing, or hold my husband's hand. Words cannot express the sadness, hurt, and feelings of missing out that I experienced during all those years in the valley, but God! Now, the trajectory had shifted, and we were back in church, worshipping the Lord Jesus together again.

Later on in the service, a third-year student named Irvin Hamilton, Jr. took everyone in that service on an impassioned journey with Jesus. He earnestly spoke about walking with Jesus and people bowed their heads and experienced the presence of the Lord. Towards the end of Irvin's preaching, his voice changed; he paused, and then declared, "Someone needs a covering." At that very moment, I opened my eyes as I stood all the way in the back of the sanctuary in the very last row. Irvin and I locked eyes, and he then said, "And it's you!" Instantly, I felt electricity bolt through my body and flew back down to the ground; my husband tried to catch me, but I was literally catapulted backward three feet. I laid out on the sanctuary floor and suddenly transported to another place with no sense of being in the church sanctuary. Light pierced darkness, the darkness completely dispelled, and pure light overcame everything; I then saw bare feet in sandals walking towards me. Then, shins and the hem of a white garment were within my arms' grasp. I reached out and clearly heard Jesus begin to speak to me. The Lord Jesus showed me photographed film negatives, single pictures in black and white, but they all were in motion, playing like a movie. I saw every single scene of my life as the Lord said, "I have broken off every negative word over your life, past, present, and future." In that moment, I knew deep within that I had been completely healed and set free. I also understood that this word wasn't just for me, but for my children and my children's children. Jesus had overcome every negative word over all our lives. I knew the words Jesus spoke were for everyone who chooses to believe. I had this sense of finality, it was finished! I had received in the depth of my being the truth that Jesus overcame all things. Sickness and disease, He has overcome; Death has been defeated because Jesus came. I have heard these words preached for years and years, but the truth of the words Jesus spoke to me as He showed me every scene of my life, illuminated my spirit in a way that it never had before. Something supernatural ignited in me. The lens I viewed human existence through wholly changed in this moment. I clearly understood the power of Jesus' presence. My spirit soared in His presence as I continued to bask in the light of His glory while laid out on the church's floor.

I had no idea five Bethel students had been praying over me the whole time while I laid out on the floor. Surprised by other voices, I was transported back, opening my eyes to see my husband's face. I locked eyes with my husband, and he initially had a concerned look, thinking that by me flying backward, hitting the floor had left me injured. However, I experienced no pain, no illness; only joy—pure freedom and *joy*! Jeff could see the joy in me, and the look on his face changed to that of peace. The students began asking me questions as I got up off the floor, and I told them of the beautiful, joyful journey I went on with Jesus just moments before.

My husband and I discussed that night's events on our way home from church. I am so thankful that the Bethel students came to Jake's House Church. The Lord powerfully moved through Irvin Hamilton, Jr. Not only had I been filled again with endless joy, but exuberant freedom that sent my spirit soaring. Jeff also received healing from the Lord that night; Jesus had removed many of the traumatic memories from our time spent in the valley.

Jeff could see the freedom on my face and the renewed hope I had for our future. I kept telling him how Jesus spoke to me and showed me that my entire life was absolutely in His care because He overcame everything. He had overcome every single negative word spoken over me, including the diagnoses given by all the doctors. Reading the Bible fills one with wisdom and knowledge; the words are like seeds that grow and blossom at various times in life. The words from the pages written on my heart had transformed from words into everlasting life. I received a profound revelation in the Lord's presence that was evident by the joy that now bubbled out of me continuously. Being filled with His joy and His Spirit in a new way fueled my very existence.

The more I laughed, the more my husband continued in his process of being healed of all trauma from the valley. The joy of the Lord was erasing those dark days that were spent endlessly weeping. The intense feelings of pain and hopelessness Jeff felt were being replaced with hope and love. Jeff's muscle memory stemmed from all those horrendous *Groundhog Day*-like events. Accustomed to pain, helplessness, and fear of me getting hurt, he reacted to life instead of *living* life. All those traumatic memories from hospitals began to come under the light of truth, and Jeff now had a new lens that he viewed me through. The painful memories started to fade as the new memories shined brightly. Each day, when he walked in the door after work, Jeff didn't have to prepare himself for the thought that I might be lying upstairs *dead*. Instead, he looked forward to greeting me and hearing all the day's stories of living and knowing all things were possible. The Lord continued to restore, renew, and refresh Jeff. He began to live again without all the trauma in the forefront of his mind. The muscle memory had been renewed!

CHAPTER 10

Carry Presence
and Live Possible

Matthew 19:26 (NKJV) says, "With men this is impossible, but with God all things are possible.'" My husband and I were now living possible. Still processing all that the miracles that the Lord had done, I pondered the future. Morning and night, I positioned myself before the Lord. A few months back on that day of absolute surrender to the Lord, when I was seeking *only* His will and laying myself at His feet, I found a place of pure joy amid the darkest hour of my existence. That moment of surrender marked me forever.

Dreams increased, and the nightmares ceased. In April 2018, I had a dream of being in India. The dream was so real; all my senses were alive. I was smelling strange new things, seeing a culture I knew nothing about, and experiencing a sense of urgency and longing to help. This dream dropped me into the third floor of a hotel, room number 123. I observed parents dressing their daughters in all white, putting bangles on their ankles and forearms, and adorning flowers in their hair. I knew something was terribly wrong. I had this urgency to rescue all these girls. The parents then proceeded to walk the girls out of the hotel courtyard across the street to the temple. Some as young as eight years old, these little girls were married off to adult men, some to the actual temple. The line of girls whose parents were forcing them to marry broke my heart. Why were they all being abandoned, married off, and sold to the temple? I cried as I ran out of the hotel to help. I woke up in tears that Sunday morning and went to church.

Jeshu Ram was speaking that morning and had just returned from an Impact Asia International trip to India. I heard of all the fantastic things Impact Asia was doing in India and learned about people I had just dreamt of the night before. After that service, I knew in my heart I had to do something about the people the Lord showed me. By the evening church service, I knew what to do. I walked up to Pastor Jeshu, handed him a check, and enrolled in Destiny International Ministry School. The next day, I started classes. Why not? What else do you do after God heals you? Through the ministry school, the Lord took me further into the path of living possible.

By May, the ministry school had a ministry trip planned to Spokane, Washington. I spoke to Jeff about going on the ministry trip. We discussed how we had not been anywhere but the hospital in the last four years; there had been no trips for vacation and no significant driving, because car rides were so painful and triggered ghastly spasms. Jeff encouraged me to go and said he would offer to be the driver for the trip. Thankfully, we owned a twelve-passenger van that could transport ministry students and all their belongings. Jeff got in touch with Jeshu Ram, the Director of Destiny International Ministry School and offered to drive. At the end of the month, off we went in the van to Spokane. This trip was the first time I left home with no oxygen, no braces, no medications, and no emergency medications or medical devices in over four years. Not only did I make the drive with zero "episodes" or setbacks, but I laughed in the joy of the Lord the whole time. Just like in Psalm 16:11, I knew that in His presence was the fullness of joy, and His joy continued to bubble out of me. Spokane has scenic pathways next to the falls, and my husband and I walked three miles around the falls. *Three miles!* Walking the falls was miraculous, since a few months earlier, the home care physical therapists would come to my home to help me walk. I had only been walking about a block or two at that time before I had to stop from pain, shortness of breath, and spams.

Now living possible by the Spirit of God, I experienced more freedom and joy than I ever imagined! There is always more with Jesus.

September arrived, and Jeff and I decided to take the leadership class together. We continued to live possible as our new way of life; we were no longer just surviving. Each day, we had a choice, and we chose to carry Jesus and live possible. Every day, we chose His joy in all things. It is possible to live joyfully. The day I started to jog brought streams of joy-filled tears. I jogged and walked three miles in December of 2018. I was very athletic in my youth; I played tennis, track, competed in triathlons, and thoroughly enjoyed running. My journey out of the depths of the valley of the shadow of death—where I was barely able to move my body—to jogging for the first time in years stirred up tears of joy. There were so many years in that valley when I cried in pain, wailed from sheer agony, and wept from prayers not yet answered, but now, the tide of tears had turned pure joy!

The victories kept coming day in and day out. In September 2019, I also heard the Lord say to clean out my house of all the remnants of sickness. Hospital home care requires a lot of stuff! My closets were full of medical devices, emergency medications, oxygen concentrators, braces, and various medical supplies. I gutted the closets and made two piles labeled "garbage" and "donate." The "garbage" pile was huge, but the "donate" pile was even more significant. I located the physician who was also in charge of an oversees medical missions' team and donated the medical equipment to physicians. All the crutches, walking boots, canes, walkers, and any other remnants of my sickness were purged from my home. All the unused medication had to be correctly disposed of, and there was a *lot* of it. The mound of medicines prescribed was delivered by mail order, and these medications just piled up. I was so thrilled to be ridding my home of all signs of sickness and disease.

The overflowing joy began bubbling in others as I ventured out. I would wake up in the morning and ask, "What do You want to do today, Lord?" I would wait on the Lord, some days longer than others, but God never fails, and He would lead me through each day. One day, while I was waiting to hear from Him, all of a sudden, I knew my task for the day: I was to return the disabled plates to the Department of Licensing. We live in a small town, and most people know you from doing business. Off I went to the DOL; I couldn't wait to return those plates. When the State of Washington issues you license plates, you also get this card that reads "permanently disabled." Who wants that label? Why on earth did I still have those plates? Upon arrival, the office was not quite open, so I had a few minutes to wait and blasted worship music in my car. His presence—the *joy* of His presence—saturated me and billowed out of me. I could not contain the joy. The doors of the DOL opened, and in I went. I flung the plates on the counter and said, "I want to return these. I no longer need them." The woman who sat behind the counter was the same person who had issued me the plates years earlier; the same woman who I had been coming to for years to get my car tabs. She saw me at the beginning of the valley; she was the one who had issued me the plates because the doctor prescribed them since I couldn't walk very far, even with oxygen. Now, I was standing before her, returning the disabled plates. She said, "No one has ever returned disabled plates before." I then pulled out my phone and began to show her pictures of me in the hospital, all the braces I no longer needed, and told her that I didn't need an oxygen backpack any longer. I also told her how the Lord Jesus healed me as I beamed with His joy. She just kept smiling at me, commented on the amazing transformation, and happily took the plates back.

The more I ventured out each day, the more I observed people's countenance change. Walking out Psalm 16:11 (NKJV) says, "In Your presence is fullness of joy." We carry king Jesus everywhere we go. Jesus lives in me, and everywhere I go, the atmosphere shifts when His kingdom is released. The joy from His presence bubbling out of me flowed in such a way that people who I came in contact with would get the giggles. Laughter is like medicine, but better! Proverbs 17:22 (NKJV) says, "A merry heart does good like medicine, But a broken spirit dries the bones." There was so much of His joy inside me that I could not contain it; it got released everywhere.

Back in April of 2019, one day, I woke up very, very early to pray, journal, and read the Word. Studying about offerings of thanksgiving had me singing praises to God. His peace and love surpassed all my understanding that morning. Thankfulness is such a key element to positioning in the presence of God. I was thanking Him for so many beautiful miracles, for leading me out of the valley of death, and for unlocking the truth of His power when He overcame the world. I continued in that position of thankfulness in my morning walk when suddenly—smack! A truck hit me, and I flew sideways off the road. I grabbed my arm and stood there in shock.

Tears came as the man screamed at me. I yelled back, "Please leave me alone." He looked like he was affected by a substance, and perhaps shouldn't have been driving. I walked back home and called my husband; Jeff immediately came home, and the worry started to flood back into him. I looked at Jeff and said, "I am not going to the hospital; I am fine." He pleaded with me to get checked out. I knew I was fine, but I went to the hospital because Jeff insisted. The week before, we had been back at my doctor's office—the doctor who wrote the letter that stated I had just a few years to live. I told him how I went off all medications, wasn't using body braces, oxygen tanks, or any assistive devices. He was very skeptical. I told him how I took his letter and put it on the altar at church, and all the pain left my body. He ordered blood tests to see where I was at. The tests would take a week or so.

While I waited in the ER for the doctor, I kept telling my husband, "I don't need to be here." I kept saying, "I am healed!" After the x-rays of my arm, shoulder, knee, and ankle, we still waited. Just then, my phone beeped, and an alert came from my doctor. I opened my electronic medical record to read the note that stated the blood tests had come back in: the tests that would show my doctor that the Lord Jesus had healed me; these tests had been run every two weeks of my life for twelve years. I read the results to my husband and burst into laughter, as all the blood work was normal. I then pulled off the heart monitor and began to get dressed. The results came back precisely as I knew in my heart; there was no sign of sickness or disease. All the tests that had always come back positive for disease were now *negative*. My doctor had no explanation on the note in my medical chart. He was puzzled. He called me an enigma. The ER doctor pressed through the curtain, and I asked him, "Can I go home now?" This ER doctor was now puzzled as well as I stood there, laughing with my husband. Thankfulness and praise that day overcame getting hit by a truck. In the past, getting whacked over by a truck would have landed me inpatient for a month or more. With God, all things are possible, and we were living possible that day. We once more walked out of the hospital with no medical intervention.

This episode to the ER was an answer to my prayers. I asked the Lord many times to help remove my chest port. I didn't need it! I wanted my last implanted chest port removed so badly. I had been walking out this process with the doctors because they typically don't just do what patients ask. I had been asking since 2018 to remove the chest port, but they wouldn't, because they still kept making me take the immunoglobulin therapy. The therapy did stop in late 2018, but the port stayed in, unused. It was now April 2019, and I desperately wanted it out! A trip to the ER answered my prayer to get into my primary care doctor. She usually had to be booked out six months in advance, but by having gone to the ER, I would now get to see her within three days. When my primary care doctor saw me, she was amazed by how I looked. I had no braces, no oxygen, had lost a lot of weight, *and* had gotten hit by a truck, but had only one little bruise on my arm. After much discussion, she finally decided to write the order to remove the port in my chest. *Praise God.* I would soon *finally* be free from all entanglements of sickness from the valley of the shadow of death.

The surgery to remove the port couldn't come soon enough for me. Surgery had not been my friend over the last twelve years; having flatlined in 2007, full-coded and stopped breathing 2013, and full-coded in June of 2017, they had to revive me time and time again. With these kinds of ghosts in your past, one wouldn't be too optimistic. However, with God, you carry His presence and live all things possible. I knew that the Word of God said in Philippians 4:13 (NKJV), "I can do all things through Christ who strengthens me," and that verse was planted deep in my innermost being. Strengthened by His joy from encountering the power of His presence in the valley of the shadow of death, I could now do all things and *live possible.*

The nurse walked into the surgery prep room and had a very puzzled look on her face. She asked several questions, then asked the same questions again. Another nurse walked in and said she was there to start an IV. I told her I didn't want any medications, and she glared back at me. Both nurses then walked out of the room. A few moments later, the surgeon came into the room with a strange look on his face. He looked me straight in the eyes and said, "We cannot do the surgery today. We do not have an adequate team in place for you to have surgery today." I replied back, "Why can't I have the surgery to remove my port today? I do not need any medication." "No medication?" he replied. I declared to the surgeon that I did not want nor would I need any medication. I happily told him how I wasn't on any medication and hadn't needed any for some time. "Well, that changes everything." Right then, the nurse proceeded to break open the IV package. "Why do I need an IV if I don't want any meds?" I asked the doctor. The surgeon looked at the nurse, told her to stop placing the IV, and had me sign a waiver because I had to consent to surgery with no medication.

I knew down in the depths of my being that I could do all things through Christ who strengthened me (Philippians 4:13, NKJV). The surgeon left to go prep and asked the nurse to walk me into the surgery suite. There were four people in the surgery suite, preparing everything for the doctor. Looking at the operating table brought back a flood of memories of previous surgeries I had in which I either completely stopped breathing or had to be revived. Instead of listening to the past's muscle memory impulses, I chose to soak in the Lord's presence, and said for all to hear, "I can do all things through Christ who strengthens me," jumping onto the surgical bed.

When the nurse cleaned the area on my skin that the surgeon would cut open to remove the port, he asked what kind of music I wanted to listen to during surgery. I requested Christian music to worship to as they did the operation to remove the chest port and catheter. Deeply implanted in my upper left chest was the port, and the catheter ran through my jugular vein into my heart. I laid there, worshiping and declaring that I could do all things through Christ.

The operation was about to begin, and I asked what the actual procedure entailed. The surgeon said, "I'm going to inject a numbing agent into the spot I am accessing to remove the port, then I will cut through any scar tissue, remove the sutures holding port to your chest, and pull the catheter out of your jugular vein." I asked because I wanted to know each step to pray for while he was working on me. I continued to talk to the surgeon as he sliced into my chest. I felt every move of that scalpel as I said, "I can do all things through Christ who strengthens me." The next thing I felt was a lot of tugging, and I asked what was happening. He told me that the scar tissue buildup was much more than anticipated and that it was becoming challenging to get through to the port. I continued to worship and declare as the doctor diligently worked. From time to time, I would ask questions about what he was doing or tell him about how amazing the last year and a half had been, giving testimony of all the Lord had done.

Suddenly, I felt a tremendous pulling in my chest. The extremely uncomfortable feeling of someone pulling on the inside your chest made me think this must be what a c-section is like (my children were all born naturally). There was tugging, pulling, more pulling, and then I felt the weirdest feeling ever. Like a creepy crawling thing that had been extracted from its home, the catheter came out of my jugular vein. The doctor then applied strong pressure on my chest. The port was out! *Praise God.*

Finally, all remnants of the valley of the shadow of death were defeated! Full of joy, I could barely lay still enough for him to stitch me up. The topical numbing agent had worn off, but I didn't care, because I could do all things through Christ who strengthened me. "Finished," said the surgeon. I sprang up off the operating table and walked out of the surgical suite back to my husband's waiting room. Surprised to see me walking immediately after surgery, he asked what happened. I exclaimed, *"It is finished!"* I then got dressed, and we walked out to leave the hospital. As we walked out, a familiar nurse who cared for me during my past inpatient hospital stays approached us and I told her how I just had my port removed because God had healed me. Stunned, she said, "We just don't see happy endings in this place." She conveyed her joy that I was now healthy and that I wouldn't be returning to the hospital. Indeed, this day marked me. To have endured a surgery with no pain meds, no muscle relaxers, no oxygen, and no kind of emergency intervention was an absolute miracle! I carried the Lord Jesus' presence into that surgical suite and walked out, demonstrating that all things are possible through Christ.

Carrying presence and living possible was part of my daily life now. After the Lord had spoken to me to "*Carry presence, live possible,*" I was now demonstrating to others by living out His words. Six months after the port removal, our wildest dreams could not have imagined where we would be heading. The church's announcement about an Impact Asia trip to India rang out like a dinner bell calling me. The dream I had about all the little girls being married off at such a young age and others just needing rescuing still burned in my mind. My husband did not share my excitement with the idea of traveling to India. We had not been on a trip abroad together since 2007, and it was now almost 2020. Our family had been very involved in missions for years before I got sick. The possibility of going on a trip halfway around the world to see such a beautiful country with vibrant people and impact youth, families, and rural communities had my heart leaping with joy. This trip was the beginning of life coming full circle.

At the first Impact Asia trip meeting, I was all in on going to India since Impact Asia International does such amazing work there with their mission of "empowering people to transform nations." My husband came along and listened, and it wasn't until he had to apply for his visa to India that he realized we were indeed going to India! We had never flown over six hours on one leg of a trip, and the only other places we had gone abroad to were in the USA, Mexico, and Peru. I couldn't contain the joy in my heart when our e-Visa from India arrived in our inboxes. What a gift to be given, to go to such a magnificent country! We were overcome with thanksgiving that God would bless us with such a trip to India.

Money? Oh yes, it takes money to go to India. I knew the Lord was calling us to go to India and believed the money would be there. The journey quickly approached, and we had only made our deposit. Jeff's love for God's word shows immensely in his craft that he has done day in and day out for the last forty years. A month before all the money was due to go on the India trip, a colleague of Jeff's had phoned him and had a conversation about us having the funds to go to India. The Friday before we were supposed to fly out for India, Jeff's colleague asked us to stop by his office. This friend and colleague handed Jeff an envelope. The Lord had spoken to Jeff's friend for over a month before he had contacted us to come by his office. We were in complete awe of the Lord's goodness! Not only had the burial clothes been ripped off of me, but the abundance of the kingdom of God was also raining down on us. Psalm 23:1 (NKJV) says, "The Lord is my shepherd, and I shall not [lack]." There was nothing we were "lacking for lacking", for the Lord provided everything we needed to go on the trip to India.

Our cup was running over; God's goodness and mercy followed us during the almost three-week trip to India in February 2020. I feared no evil would come because I carried His presence; the power of the Lord's presence. The trip on the airplane further demonstrated the work Jesus had done in my body. As I boarded the flight with the team, the goodness of God flooded my spirit. There I was, on a plane with no oxygen, no medications, and no assistance devices. The air travel time was twenty-four hours, and I did not get short of breath once. Two years before, I was on oxygen 24/7 due to my lungs' damage from collapsing during previous surgeries. In the past, flight attendants used to monitor me because my oxygen levels would drop so low on flights that they almost turned the plane around, but God! I was now travelling halfway around the world to such a magnificent country. My cup ran over with love. We experienced so many miracles on the trip to India; our hearts burst with joy. I was so thankful, for the Lord had strengthened me, breathed His life into me, and restored me!

The journey through the valley of the shadow of death and out the other side taught me how to *carry presence* and *live possible*. I live in the Lord's joy because of His presence. Psalm 16:11 (NKJV) says In Your presence is fullness of joy." It's been almost three years since that day I completely surrendered and cried out to God to do something: either take me to heaven or heal me. On that day, the Lord breathed His life into me, rose me up off my sickbed, tore off the grave clothes that were about to bury me, and filled me with His peace, strength, and joy. Now, every day, I *carry presence* and *live possible!*

The following are my photographs of
Carrying Presence and Living Possible

This picture is of the homecare health supplies that I no longer needed. All of it was given back to a physician who also oversees a medical mission abroad.

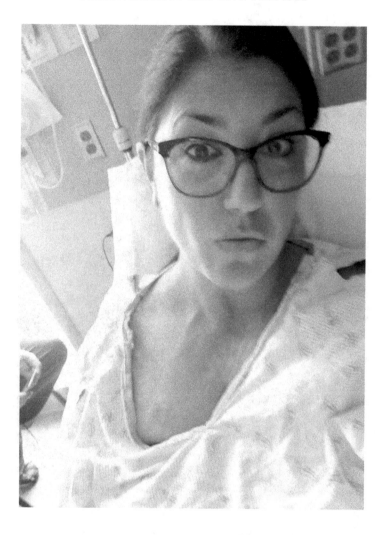

Pre-surgery picture of my chest port removal surgery in 2019. The doctors finally agreed to remove the chest port after I hadn't used it for over a year and a half. I no longer needed any medication through the port.

After surgery. No more port! This surgery was an absolute miracle: no medications, no IV, and no interventions. The surgeon opened me up, removed the port, and stitched me back up without even an IV in place. I got up off the operating table and walked out of the hospital; they didn't even take my blood pressure.

Febuary 2020 in Kancheepuram, India.

This picture is me in 2020: wife, mother of five, and grandmother of nine. "In Your presence is fullness of joy" (Psalm 16:11, NKJV). I live in the joy of His presence, completely healed of all pain, sickness, and disease.

CHAPTER 11

Testimonials

The following are letters written by friends, family, pastors. I have also included excerpts from my medical records. The letters tell of their encounters with me over the years before I got sick, during the years spent in the valley of the shadow of death, and after walking out the other side of the valley, *living possible*. I am so thankful and blessed by all who took the time to write a letter of testimony about what they witnessed the Lord do in my life.

Letter from Pastors Keith and Karmin Kippen:

I have come to know Jeff and Lisa Lancaster over many years. I first met them at a church in Marysville, WA, called Judah Praise Center, where dear friends of ours, James and Kathy Berkley, were pastors. I was on staff at a local church nearby, and we would often get together with Pastor James and other pastors in Marysville for prayer and fellowship. Falling in love with James and Kathy was easy, and before long, our ministries were enjoying fellowship together, and James would often have our ministry team and me come to Judah Praise Center.

JPC is where I first met Jeff and Lisa. Like so many of the families at Judah Praise Center, Jeff and Lisa were full of joy, loved the Lord, and had a passion for His Kingdom! I witnessed firsthand their love to pray for people and see people healed, saved, and set free. I also saw their love for missions, going into the world, sharing the love of God, and preaching the gospel. Our wonderful relationship with Pastor James and Kathy flourished in the late 1990s and early 2000s leading to 2007. In September of 2007, Jake's House

Church was born, and Karmin, myself, and the Jake's House family asked Pastor James Berkley to be one of our board of directors for the church. We were tremendously honored by him being our first board member, and his faithful support and encouragement much blessed Jake's House! Sadly, on December 27, 2009, Pastor James Berkley died suddenly of a massive heart attack while preaching his life message on reconciliation.

I remember right before James's death, Jeff and Lisa had significantly been impacted by a mission trip to Peru with Pastor James. Along the same timeline, shortly after that trip, Lisa started having some severe health challenges, starting with a battle with cancer. Then, about a year after James's death, Jeff and Lisa started attending Jake's House Church. I think it was probably a natural fit for them because of our close relationship with Kathy and James.

During those beginning years of attending Jake's House Church, their commitment was very sporadic. Though I felt they wanted to be there, and especially to have their kids there, it seemed like it was very much a battle. I believe it was because of many family and health issues that we did not see much of Jeff and Lisa for those first few years.

I remember it was around 2016 when we begin to see Jeff and Lisa a bit more. I know it was very difficult for Lisa, because at this stage, she was really battling a couple of autoimmune diseases that were totally crippling her with pain. I believe it was our annual Week of Refreshing in January 2017, and things were intensifying, when Joy, Lisa's birth mom, brought up Lisa for ministry because one of our guest speakers wanted to pray for the two of them. I remember the severity of Lisa's pain and the challenges it presented for her to make it to our conference. At some point during the conference, I remember her pulling me aside and talking to me about wanting to come to all the services, but many people were touching her and greeting her, and it was too physically painful for her to bear.

Later that year, Jeff gave me a call to come to pray for Lisa in the hospital as soon as I possibly could. It just so happened that I was in the very same hospital ministering to another family, so I came right over. Lisa had coded from full respiratory failure earlier, and the doctors almost lost her. Jeff was by her bedside, tremendously concerned and scared. When I got there, I could sense a bit of relief in Jeff, but Lisa was not very coherent. We did have a powerful prayer time, though, and I sensed the Lord was keeping Lisa here.

Fast-forwarding to the fall and the end of November 2017, the Lord had me begin to declare that 2018 was going to be the best year of our lives for the Jake's House Family! I think that Lisa had heard me give these words initially online, or maybe through her husband Jeff, because for much of the second half of that year, Lisa needed home care. Either way, Lisa found her way to a service Sunday morning, and heard me repeat the word of the Lord again: that 2018 was going to be the best year of our lives! I remember her grabbing me after the service. I remember a boldness coming on me, and personally declaring this word from the Lord over Lisa. Then, a couple of weeks later, Lisa came to the first night of our annual conference, the Week of Refreshing, in January 2018. After the service, she handed me a doctor's letter that basically said she was not going to live past 2018. I remember her saying, "This letter is not mine; it's not for me." She laid that letter on the altar, and I agreed with her in the spirit, but we knew that it was more than just a letter or a doctor's declaration that was being laid down. The Lord was speaking to her that this whole long season of attack was over!

A couple of months later, Lisa signed up for our school of ministry. We were beginning to see Jeff and Lisa all the time at church, laughing and smiling! I remember at the end of the school year, they went on a ministry trip to Spokane, and it was so glorious to see her walking out her healing and seeing the both of them fully coming alive!

In the fall, now the two of them were signed up for our ministry school, and we all saw the miraculous improvement in Lisa's body and life! Then, I believe sometime in the spring or late winter of 2019, Lisa and Jeff gave a testimony before the church of her complete healing. It was so impactful to our people, because many of them knew Jeff and Lisa and what they had been walking through for years. Lisa's brother's family also attended our church all this time, as well as other family members and friends who knew them intimately. However, probably one of the most impactful pieces of their testimony was the pictures of the large tub of medications and multiple braces that Lisa has been using over the last almost ten years.

It has been such a joy to see Jeff and Lisa living out God's promise and faithfulness. They have been actively involved in our church family, and they have even helped Karmin and me with our tile work for our new home! However, probably the greatest thing to see is a full-circle journey of them going back on the mission field this last February to India! The fruit of God's glorious testimony continues to fall off the tree of their lives!

Much love,

Pastors Keith & Karmin Kippen
Lead Pastors, Jake's House Church

Letter from Jeff Lancaster, my husband:

My name is Jeff, and I am the most blessed because Lisa Lancaster is my wife. When I first met Lisa and got to know her, I had never encountered someone like her. Though she had a life in which most of us would struggle to have a positive outlook, she never let herself be a victim of circumstances.

Lisa's way of life was a constant pursuit of knowledge, especially about God and faith; she had a never-ending supply of energy, which the Lord knew she needed with five little ones to raise. She helped to open my mind to experience living, not just to work hard and to strive through life.

I guess the most beautiful things about the Lord bringing Lisa and me together was Lisa being an on-fire, spirit-filled Christian and me learning that God really wants to have a relationship with me and that Christianity is not just a religion.

The Lord did prepare us for what was to come; of course, that is easy to say now from the other side. In 2007, I got the opportunity to go on a mission trip to Peru with my pastor and a large group of youth, one being our youngest son. It was not easy to leave Lisa because this was when she started experiencing some strange health problems, but she wanted nothing more for my son and me to have this experience. Before this trip, we had gone on family mission trips to Mexico and within the USA and I had done some building mission trips.

The Peru trip was so full of God's supernatural power. We saw the Lord move in each of us. I saw so many people healed in the blink of an eye. My faith was so lifted up! I thought to myself, When I return home, Lisa will be healed, and life will go back to the way it was before. However, God doesn't go backward, and that's not the way it was. What I witnessed for more than a decade is one of the strongest people I have ever met.

I thought I would share a small sample of the prayers and conversations between the Lord and me during that difficult time:

Lord, I love You and I thank You. You trusted me to be a soulmate with Lisa, and I know that with just a thought, You could make her well. Thank You, Lord. Amen.

Father, I praise Your name. Thank You, Jesus, for Your sacrifice. By Your stripes, we are healed; please heal Lisa, my precious wife.

God, You know what I am asking for. Do You get tired of me asking? I hope not. I try to be strong for her, but it is so hard to watch her suffer.

Jesus, You said we should fast and pray, but if I fast, I won't have the strength to help her up the stairs or stay up and watch her breath in case she needs more oxygen. Lord, what is all this for? What can I do? I am so helpless. Please stop the suffering.

Lord, I am starting to get mad. I don't want to be mad; I am not an angry person. The doctors try, but they are as helpless as I am, and what some doctors do hurts Lisa so much.

Lord, I am not going to ask You to heal Lisa anymore. I am only going to thank You for healing her and giving us a future together.

Lord, I cannot pray today.

Father, here I am again. I am sorry. I know how much You love Lisa and You're waiting for her to be with You, but I am selfish; I need her to stay with me longer. We didn't have enough time together; we still have things we wanted to do. Please end her suffering one way or another. I trust Your perfect will. Amen.

All praise and glory be to You, Jesus Thank You for healing Lisa. I am overwhelmed. I am so excited for our future together.

Lord, I am sorry, but I don't know why I am still sad. I want to be filled with the joy that Lisa now has since You healed her. It is hard to hear her great testimony because all I remember is the pain and fear. Thank You for Your joy that is filling me. Amen.

Since that last prayer, Lisa and I have had opportunities to give testimonies of this tremendous miracle. Seeing hope rise up in people has filled me with more joy than I could have ever imagined. I pray that this book of testimony gives joy to whoever reads it. God bless you.

Letter from Cody Lancaster, my youngest son:

Growing up in a faith-filled home with five siblings and two loving parents made for a very busy childhood. Between sports, church events, family events, and everything else, my mother made sure everyone got what they needed and got to where they needed to be. She was a stay-at-home mother for most of my young life, always putting others before herself.

It was when I was beginning high school when things really started to change. When my mom started this journey with her illness, it was a very scary and confusing time. Watching someone you care about fall extremely ill in front of you gives you a very hopeless feeling; you feel powerless. However, my mom always remained faithful and hopeful.

As time went on and my mom's illness progressed, my parents were rarely at their home due to twenty-plus day hospital stays. I would try to help my dad around his house so he could be with her longer. I also remember getting calls from my dad asking me to go by the house if I wasn't working to check on my mom because she was not answering her phone. That fear caused by uncertainty is a paralyzing feeling.

I also recall bringing my kids to see my mom at the hospital, thinking to myself that I did not want this to be the last memory my kids have of their grandma. Even through all the sickness, pain, restlessness, and hard times my mom went through, she still had faith. She proclaimed strength even when she didn't feel strong. She was always asking how she could help, even when sitting in a hospital bed.

The power of faith is such an incredible thing! My mom proclaimed her healing and held onto the promise that God had for her life. *God follows through.* God fulfilled His promise in my mom's life.

Life today is incredible. To see my mom do everything she wants to do in life without pain is so amazing. My kids got to witness how faith works! Our God is a God of restoration, not condemnation. My mom's journey is a prime example that our God heals and restores. God makes *all* things work together for His and our good.

Be blessed,
Cody Lancaster

Letter from Haley Lancaster, my daughter-in-law:

I met Lisa six short years ago and quickly learned that her life revolved around going to the doctor and getting infusions. She was having trouble doing simple life tasks. Lisa would occasionally babysit for me, but it was hard to schedule with her because of the weekly doctor and emergency room visits. After marrying her son Cody, I was more and more aware of all the health issues she was struggling with, and we would visit her on her twenty to forty-day hospital stays. We would have to help her around the house and with their animals so that Jeff could stay with her. We tried to help Jeff as much as we could when he would try to work.

Lisa always has had the best heart and would do everything she could to help me with our now four daughters, but still, it was hard to do, as her life really orbited around being sick. Fast-forwarding about three years into knowing her, she became very involved in church, which changed her life! When I had met her in the thick of the chaos of her being ill and consumed with that, I don't remember her going to church. God prompted her to go back, and because of that calling, she obeyed was healed. I remember when she stopped wearing her metal hand and finger braces and didn't need her hearing aids. She was able to load around the kids. Her appointments went from multiple days a week to almost never. It was night and day! I had really never seen such a change in someone overnight and more and more as she has continued to follow the path that God put her on! I am so thankful to have her help as a super involved grandma, and for her influence on our children as a testimony to them!

Letter from Josh Omlid, my brother:

My name is Josh Omlid, and I am Lisa Lancaster's brother. We live near each other, and I have witnessed the miracle that has transformed her life.

Many years before her getting sick, her life was focused on excitement to finish her education and start another career in a more specialized field that she had been pursuing. When the opportunity came, she was so thankful and happy to start this new position and fulfill her pursuit. I remember visiting her at the office, doing the normal activities of life that people do when they have their health. Lisa was no stranger to dealing with health issues. After battling thyroid cancer, all eyes were on the future, and we thought the worst was behind us.

As Lisa's health began to decline, I remember the struggle she had as she continued working. We were tired—*exhausted*, in fact, with so many questions and so few answers. As the decline continued to progress, I remember her relaying to me her desire for her kids not to know how bad things were getting and then had become. I remember visiting her when she could no longer work and was having frequent blood transfusion treatments for what had now become a small window of relief. Her body was now racked with pain; one had to take care not to hug her and take extra precautions about seeing her so as to not introduce any type of virus that could impact her weakened immune system. I remember visiting her at the hospital. Her hope was in the Lord, yet it was challenging to find joy in what seemed like only despair.

When Lisa was healed, that despair was cast off her, and her countenance changed. The weight of years of both physical and mental anguish, which had taken their toll, were no longer welcome; she was free. Her outlook and demeanor shifted quickly and continued to brighten as she was able to go from an isolated life due to the impact of her illness to living again. This transformation was massive. Hope was fulfilled, and with it, joy had come. Lisa's future is brighter than ever; thank You, Jesus!

Letter from Kristen Hoidal, my friend:

My husband Kevin and I first met Jeff and Lisa in the late 1990s. We lived in a small town in western Washington called Stanwood. We met at Stanwood Foursquare Church. I had just had my second out of four children. Lisa, only being a year older than me, had finished having all of her children. Her youngest was only a couple of years older than my oldest and was involved in many of the same church activities; we soon became friends.

The thing I remember most about Lisa in those early years was her unending energy. I was only in my late twenties and had felt that I had a good amount of energy. We used to go running together. She was up early with her husband to have coffee with him before going off to work every morning. Also, she was homeschooling five kids, living on a farm, doing farm things, doing things with friends and family, watching people's kids without being paid, serving at the church, working with the church's junior high youth group, and having church camps at her house during the summer for the pre-school *and* grade school kids at our church. She even went off and got her bachelor's degree.

She was just always non-stop, and on top of it all, Lisa and her husband Jeff loved the Lord deeply. The power of the Holy Spirit rested on them both. Bible studies and prayer groups were all par for the course for the Lancaster family. When my husband Kevin and I bought our first house, they came over and blessed our home, praying over our family and our house. I remember Jeff and Kevin walking around our house, putting stakes in all four corners of our property, declaring the property for the Lord. They are the poster child family for what a young Christian family should look like.

It all started very slowly at first. I remember Lisa was talking about feeling fatigued and feeling just not right. Lisa felt that something was wrong with her body, and she was eating extra healthy to help compensate. She started reading up on health issues and checking into her family health history, so she decided to go to the doctor. This was the beginning of the unending doctor's appointments and quite frankly bizarre physical ailments that started to assault Lisa. I remember the day she told me the doctors said she had thyroid cancer and wanted to put radioactive dye into her. She did not want it. This was the first of many refusals Lisa had to give to the doctors who were declaring sickness over her body. Our relationship started to change very slowly as her illness progressed. It was no longer, "Hey, do you want to go for a run?" or "Do you want to go get lunch?" It was now, "What did the doctors say?", "When is your next doctor's appointment?", "When does that test come back?", and "What bizarre thing is happening to your body now?" I remember one of the first bizarre things that was happening to her was that her skin would heat up to the point where she was too hot to touch, and she'd have to take a cold shower just to cool her skin down. The sicker Lisa got, the less we hung out, which makes sense; she wasn't feeling well, and any extra time she had was beginning to get eaten up by more and more needed doctor's appointments. She was also finishing up her degree and starting a fulltime job.

As things progressed, she got worse and worse; she eventually had to be on medical leave from her job. Fast forward a couple of years, and I hardly ever saw her anymore. Lisa has had her thyroid removed, was diagnosed with cancer, had some weird brain things going on, and had been diagnosed with celiac disease on top of other weird eating issues. Her joints were also starting to freak out on her. There were times when she couldn't move, times where she could move but not walk, and times where she was just in constant unending pain. I saw her on her good days, which were getting further and further apart.

I remember one time seeing her at Haggen's grocery store in town. She hadn't seen me, so I snuck up behind her and reached out and grabbed her to scare her and say "hi." I thought she was going to kill me. Up until this point, I didn't know Lisa had stopped being able to be touched. I knew at various times it hurt for her to be touched, but I hadn't realized the extent and my coming up to her, grabbing her from the back and surprising her had sent her body into week-long spasms of pain. I had been hurt by my friend's death glare and hurtful reaction to my fun surprise way of saying "hi." I had no idea what I had done. We drifted further apart. We were still friends, but there would be months between seeing each other, then years.

One of the last times I remember seeing Lisa, we were at a dinner somewhere, and she had started to wear capes instead of jackets or coats for warmth. They were more comfortable because she still couldn't stand being touched, and the tight fit of jackets and coats bothered her. My friend also started wearing what looked like funny-looking rings over her fingers, knuckles, and wrists because of the pain in her joints. The medication she was taking had made her body swell up to the point where she was almost unrecognizable. She said the medication she took made her have something called "moon face"; she looked just like it sounds. Lisa said she didn't like people staring, and she stopped going out in public much. A few years later, my husband Kevin ran into Jeff at another grocery store in town he asked Jeff how Lisa was doing; Jeff told him, "Not very good," and that they were hoping that Lisa would live long enough to see the birth of one of their grandchildren. It would be three years before I would see my friend again.

After sixteen years in the same church, my husband and I felt the Lord telling us to move to a different church. So, we did—by the way, we still love Stanwood Foursquare, it's a great church. We had been attending our new church, Jake's House Church, for seven years when who shows up one Sunday morning but my dear sweet friends Jeff and Lisa Lancaster! It was awesome to see them after such a long time. Of course, my first urge was to hug my long-lost friends, but I wouldn't go anywhere near Lisa. I remembered what happened the last time I touched her and wanted her to feel safe. Her moon face was gone, and she looked good, but she was still wearing capes and had even more of that strange jewelry on her hands and wrists, and she had braces on other parts of her body. After talking with her and Jeff, things were still the same; just much worse: endless doctor appointments turned into countless specialist appointments. Lisa took it up a notch with endless hospital stays. She had surgery after surgery and procedure after procedure and medication on top of medication. She was now considered to be in special groups; only 150 people in the world were known to have her condition, and another group had a two percent survival rate. There were now "fun" group sayings like "no one has ever seen anything like this before" that applied to Lisa. My poor friends. Hadn't they suffered enough?

However, I was glad to see my friends. I was happy to see them; even through all of the sicknesses and struggle, Lisa and Jeff still were loving and serving the Lord. I was glad they were going to Jake's House Church. I knew this church was different; it had changed my life and brought me deeper in the Lord. The Holy Spirit was there! I knew this was the right place for Jeff and Lisa to be.

I wish I could remember the exact date, but I can't. However, I will never forget that day. I've known Jeff and Lisa Lancaster for over twenty years. For almost half of those years, I've witnessed Lisa's illness and the suffering she and her family have had to go through.

Since they had started attending Jake's House church, I talked with Jeff and Lisa occasionally, and one of the last things I re-member her telling me was that her doctor had written her a letter saying she'd be dead in three years, that there was nothing else they could do for her. There was no more medical way to treat her; she had exhausted all known modern-day medical remedies and should just go home and wait to die. I have never once heard Jeff or Lisa agree with what the doctors have said through all of this. It has always been, "The doctors have said I have this, but Jesus is my healer," or "The doctors have said this, but God says this." Throughout this whole ordeal, we have always prayed that God would heal Lisa. Jeff and Lisa have always stood in faith, saying God would heal her, but this was the final word of the doctors: there would be nothing else left to do.

I will never forget the day I saw her healed. I was in church saying "hi" to some friends, when this person comes up behind me and gives me this great big bear hug, maybe even lifted me off the floor. I turn around to greet whoever it was that was hugging me, and to my eternal shock and surprise, my friend Lisa Lancaster gave me one of the biggest hugs of my life! I couldn't believe it! I stood there with my mouth gaping open, just staring at her. Here was my friend standing before me: whole, no capes, no weird silver jewelry, no body braces, and she was touching me!

I couldn't believe it! My friend, whom I hadn't touched in years; my friend, whom I had hurt so badly so many years ago by a simple hug, now hugged me! Lisa was standing there with this massive grin on her face, shaking her head up and down, telling me "yes" to my unspoken question. I knew that was her way of telling me she was healed! The Lord had healed her! I couldn't stop hugging her after that; I just kept going back to hug her, stepping back and then hugging her again and again just because I could! The Lord has healed her completely, not just a little; my friend Lisa is whole! Jesus had healed her!

Letter from Lola Neal, my friend:

How exciting this journey of healing has been; what an exciting thing God has done in this woman of God.

I met Jeff, Lisa's husband, at a job site in 2005. Upon talking with him, he shared with me what had been happening in their lives. I said, "I must meet this woman; there is something very special about her."

I did finally get to meet her. She was so full of life all about her family. Shortly after, however, her health began to fail. One thing after another, her health became worse, as the treatment failed or something put her in the hospital for a month or more. When she did come home, she would have to sleep downstairs because she couldn't climb the stairs.

I remember the day that healing came. Jeff had called and told me he had to leave her alone. He had to go to work, and he didn't want to leave her alone. He said, "I don't even know if she will be alive when I get home." I hadn't realized things had gotten so bad, and I didn't really think so much about what he had said since they had been going through this for so long. The Lord gave me a word for them on November 21, 2017 from Psalm 21.

God did exactly what was written in that Psalm in her life. The next time I saw her, she was brimming with life, all smiles and laughter. Even to this day, when you see her, she is filled with so much joy, peace, and laughter. What a beautiful testimony of God's healing.

What totally blesses me is how God joined our hearts together even before I met Lisa; even before "worse and worse." Jeff would take her to the hospital to get treatments, then head to work all day. Then, after work, he would pick her back up. Other times, he would stay with her. On some of those occasions, he would ask me to come to clean the house, mainly the kitchen, because one of their kids would cook something that Lisa was allergic to, and it would need to be cleaned before she got home. I could feel the weight of what was going on in their home. There was sadness, fear, and uncertainty, and yet they were believing in God for complete healing.

I remember when I was in Everett with them one day, her body started going into spasms for what seemed to be ten or fifteen minutes; it took her all she could do to keep from falling on the floor. I remember seeing her at church, barely moving. No one could touch her because it would cause her extreme pain. My heart was so sad for her and Jeff; to watch someone you care about be in so much pain. I remember the port that they had put in to help when she became ill. When Jeff would tell me what was going on in their lives, God would give me scriptures to counter what they were going through. It was as if God had given me open access to heaven to pray and share His will with them. I know now that is exactly what He had done.

Letter from Amanda Munson, my friend:

Lisa is such a testimony to the process of freedom and the momentum of grace as it moves over a willing heart, bringing healing. Jesus has walked with her through it all, and what a beautiful process it has been!

I met Lisa when I was a teenager over twenty years ago and have watched the many seasons of life unfold for her and her family. At the time, she was a young mother raising five kids and was completely devoted to them. She and her husband, Jeff, served in their local church and had such a heart for the Lord. They took mission trips and loved to worship and pray for people.

At one point, I remember running into Lisa and hearing about how she had become a teacher and was working full time and loving it. I had heard she had some health problems that were unresolved and starting to become a challenge. What followed would be years and years of health challenges, medical interventions, and eventually, a disability diagnosis. There were times over the following years that we heard Lisa was in the hospital, was having surgery, or was seeing a new specialist. I knew she was no longer able to work and how disappointing that was for her. There was so much limitation on Lisa because of her health.

A friend asked me if I would go to Lisa's house to cut and color her hair. I had recently quit my job at the salon I had been working at and was homeschooling my kids. My friend told me that Lisa was so sick she couldn't leave her house, making a trip to the salon impossible. When I arrived, I was surprised to see firsthand how the disease had ravaged her body. Lisa was in near constant pain, and she could not walk very far. Her breathing was labored. There was a literal pile of medications on the counter, and she often would need to use her inhaler while I was there. As I colored Lisa's hair, we talked about what her life was like now and how she was coping. The prognosis she lived with was one of a life cut short. She had recently been in the ICU, and it was a miracle that she was even still alive. There was so much heaviness over her as she expressed just how difficult this was for her and her family.

Even in the midst of it all, for Lisa, it always came back to Jesus. She clung to him.

We would talk for hours about what God had been doing in our lives, sharing scriptures and testimonies. I had been radically healed in 2015 and felt like Jesus had given me my life back. Lisa listened to my own testimony with faith, we cried, and she shared prophetic encounters she'd had with the Lord out of her journal. Her tender heart toward the Lord and her love for His presence was always profound, but there was a lot of pain. We talked about all the challenges over the years and how that affected us. Lisa was honest, and I appreciated that. A season began of me visiting every few months to cut and color Lisa's hair in her home.

I would describe the following year as one of both sudden and gradual healing. We saw Lisa pressing into the presence of God at our local church. She and Jeff opened their hearts to this community of faith. She had powerful encounters with Jesus and was beginning to heal. Her focus seemed to change from injury and past hurts to freedom and forgiveness. Every time I saw her, she looked better, healthier, and happier. Lisa has the best laugh, and it seemed to bubble up out of her every time I saw her. She was bursting with testimony and joy. Medications were dropped. She started walking and had her stamina return; it was beautiful.

To see Lisa as she is today, serving on the mission field, in good health, and full of joy is a true miracle! There are keys to the process of healing in her testimony that will release breakthroughs for others. Her life is one bought back by the love of Jesus, flowing with fresh oil, and I have been privileged to watch it unfold. For Jeff and Lisa, this is just the beginning of the Lord using them for His glory.

Letter from Jeshu Ram, President of Impact Asia International:

My first memory of Lisa was in the fall of 2017, when she and Jeff walked into the church and she was on oxygen. My first thought was how I wanted to see God heal this woman completely. A few months later, during our annual conference in January of 2018, I saw Lisa at the altar, seeking God for a breakthrough. Despite all her considerable pain and extensive physical restrictions, she attended most of the services that week. The doctors had lost hope and could not see her living much longer, but she and Jeff were contending for her breakthrough. She was receiving her healing by faith, with Jeff never leaving her side and believing with her. A few weeks later, I saw her again, this time without the oxygen tank. She was not the same woman. I could see the miracle taking place from the inside out.

One Sunday, she came to me after I had shared testimonies from a trip to India. She shared in detail a dream she had about this young girl wearing a white Indian outfit in a hotel. She saw God rescuing this young girl from her situation and healing her. At that moment, I felt God say that she was going to go to India with us. She laughed and said, "That would be a miracle; I don't know about that." I said, "God can do miracles," and asked her to write that dream in her journal.

It was so encouraging to me and everyone in the church to witness the miracle of Lisa. There was so much joy and life that was coming out of her. It was releasing hope and breakthroughs for others' conditions and circumstances. She started attending all our prayer meetings and serving in the church. She was a walking miracle!

Jeff and Lisa started coming to our leadership school on Tuesday nights. In that class, Lisa was asked to write a five-year vision for her life. It was a challenging process for her to dream again after what she had been through. With Jeff's help and the Holy Spirit, she started to dream again. Part of that dream was her going to the nations and writing a book. She did not know how it was all going to happen; she just believed God!

In February of 2020, Jeff and Lisa went to India with us for two weeks. During that time, I witnessed a glimpse of God's design and purpose for Jeff and Lisa's life and destiny. God used them to impact many lives through her miraculous story. There were healings and deliverances; there was hope and joy, and they made such an impact in India. Also, they met and continue to minister healing and hope to the girl she dreamt about. That girl is their spiritual daughter today!

Lisa and Jeff have ignited the hearts of India's young and old with faith, hope, love, and power of the Holy Spirit with Lisa's life and story. They are still discipling pastors and families in India and other nations and advancing the kingdom God in this earth.

When I look at her life, I see the message of God turning a mess into a miracle!

His son,
Jeshu Ram,
President, Impact Asia International

Excerpts taken from my medical record:

Progress note signed by Paul T. McBride, MD
4/2/2019 7:32 AM

Lisa comes in. She showed me remarkable transition. Since last year (01/13/2018), she has basically not been on any medication. She has resolved all of her underlying diseases, and it would appear her autoimmune is in remission.

Plan: I told Lisa I am sort of at a loss to explain how she is in remission, but I do not want to discount this. I would like to get all of the foreign bodies out of her, including her port, and get her off as many or all of her medications if possible, but will not make that decision until I see her labs. Ordered Labs today.

Progress Notes signed by Paul T. McBride, MD
1/15/2020 2:00 PM

Lisa comes back for annual follow-up and she is just elated. She says all of her disease is gone, she says all of her symptoms are gone, her joint symptoms are gone, and her immunoglobulin levels are maintaining. She has no liver or spleen or anything involved and she says even her cataracts have gone away. So, she is a total enigma to me, I do not know how any of this has happened. I am excited for her, but I am still un-clear how all these things have occurred. So, at this point, it would appear that her connective tissue disease has resolved, her vasculitis has resolved, her stiff person syndrome has re-solved and her hearing loss she says is even better. But at this point, I do not know how any of this had happened and I am just happy for her. She is going to be traveling to India.

Plan: Sero, screen Lisa today to see if she needs any vaccines for measles, mumps, chickenpox, or rubella, and then vacci-nate her for hepatitis A and B for her upcoming trip. I just remarked that I am very happy that her disease turned out the way it did; I still have no idea how that happened. —Paul McBride, MD

08/05/2020

You are still a pleasant enigma to me in that I don't know what made you better, but I am just glad that it did. —Paul McBride, MD

CHAPTER 12

Reflections from the Shadow

I read the Word, journaled, prayed, and prayer-walked for hours every morning since the Lord healed me. I had the pleasure of staying home and just soaking in the Lord's presence every morning; I give many thanks to my husband, who was steadfastly providing and covering me with his blessing. I learned a lot through the twelve-year journey and took away so much more than what the enemy stole from me in the valley of the shadow of death. I remembered the words from Psalm 16:11 (NKJV): "In His presence is fullness of joy." In His Presence, I am continually filled with His joy and His strength that burns in me to *"carry presence, live possible."* This phrase is what God spoke to me when asking Him about my vision statement. When the Lord dropped those four words into me, I deeply understood what took place when he healed me. I received a new lens to clearly see His kingdom. We carry king Jesus' presence everywhere we go; His presence shifts atmospheres, His presence moves mountains, His presence changes the impossible to possible. Listed below are revelatory takeaways I learned from the valley of the shadow of death. I pray these reflections bring hope and encouragement.

The first big takeaway from this journey through the valley of the shadow of death is that God did not create me to live in sickness; **He made me to live in communion with Him.** John 14:16 (NKJV) says, "And I will pray the Father, and He will give you another Helper, that He may abide with you forever." Relying on the Spirit of God to lead in all things is vital. How do I live in communion with Jesus? Through *prayer*—talking to Him every day. Including Jesus in every moment and having praise on my lips and thanksgiving flowing out of my heart fosters an atmosphere of His presence throughout the day. "Pray without ceasing, in everything give thanks; for this is the will of God in Christ Jesus for you" (1 Thessalonians 5:17-18, NKJV). Journaling what I am thankful for and giving the Lord praise for all things fosters His presence, as well as a constant awareness of choosing to abide in the vine; Jesus is our source of life. Yes, it is possible to live in the Lord's presence all day long.

The second takeaway is to **always speak life.** Everything that comes out of my mouth is to speak life. Proverbs 18:21 (NKJV) says, "Death and life are in the power of the tongue, and those who love it will eat its fruit." Speaking life changes the atmosphere. Fostering an atmosphere of life in my home helped me see all things that could possibly come to be. Right after the Lord healed me, I only allowed family and friends to speak life. I did not allow any negative comments about other people about themselves or the day's events; only words of life were spoken in my home and around me. The fruit of speaking life was very evident. A statement from Romans 4:17 (NKJV) says, "God who gives life to the dead and calls those things which do not exist as though they did." The first thing to come out of my mouth affected what transpired. For example, I declared to my husband that everything would be okay after being told the port pierced my heart and that I should be dead. I did not receive that word; I believed and spoke life over myself. The fruit of speaking life that day was walking out of the hospital with no intervention and witnessing to others that with God, all things are possible. Speaking life, declaring the Word of God overcame the negative reports.

The third takeaway from the valley is to **receive all that God has.** God is good all the time. Psalm 23:6 (NKJV) says, "Surely goodness and mercy **shall** follow me All the days of my life, And I will dwell in the house of the Lord Forever." I received strength. I believed God,

149

and I received it. According to Mark 5:36 (NKJV), Jesus says, "Do not be afraid; only believe." Only believe! Yes, all things are possible with God. Receiving is an action that is more than just hearing a word; it takes effort on our part. We drink in His Spirit: "For by one Spirit we were all baptized into one body—whether Jews or Greeks, whether slaves or free—and have all been made to drink into one Spirit" (1 Corinthians 12:13, NKJV). When we believe and drink, the fruit is the flowing of the Spirit of God. In John 7:37-38 (NKJV), Jesus says, "If anyone thirsts, let him come to Me and drink. He who believes in Me, as the scripture has said, out of his heart will flow rivers of living water." When we choose to drink from Jesus, who is the living water, we never thirst, we have no lack, and we receive the abundance of heaven on earth.

The fourth takeaway is that **carrying His presence changes the atmosphere**; carry king Jesus everywhere. 1 John 4:4 (NKJV) says, "You are of God, little children, and have overcome them, because He who is in you is greater than he who is in the world." *He that is in me is greater!* Nothing is impossible, and atmospheres change when we carry His presence. His light pierces the dark places. Psalm 23:4 (NKJV) says, "Yea, though I walk through the valley of the shadow of death, I fear no evil; For You are with me; Your rod and Your staff, they comfort me." Jesus strengthened me in the valley of the shadow of death; His presence filled me with peace like still waters. Psalm 23:2 (NKJV) says, "He makes me to lie down in green pastures; He leads me beside the still waters." The Lord did not leave me alone in the valley of the shadow of death; He walked me through it. His presence pierced the darkness and gave me a new vision to clearly see His kingdom on earth as it is in heaven. With this new lens, the sickness did not overshadow me; Jesus anointed my head with oil and filled me with His presence. His kingdom is released when we choose to carry His presence and release it through righteousness, peace, and joy in the Holy Spirit. Romans 14:17 (NKJV) says, "for the kingdom of God is not eating and drinking, but righteousness and peace and joy in the Holy Spirit."

The fifth takeaway is that **the oil of the Lord is vital.** Psalm 23:5 (NKJV) says, "You prepare a table for me in the presence of my enemies; You anoint my head with oil; My cup runs over." The Lord showed me through this new lens that as believers, we are anointed daily with oil from the Lord. Every day, the Lord pours out fresh oil that we position to receive by setting our hearts on Him and waiting on Him. Furthermore, the physical act of anointing your forehead consecrates and sets you apart for Jesus and the Spirit of God to move through you and lead you throughout the day. It's a constant communion; an abiding in His presence with a willing heart. To receive the oil of the Lord means to live in the abundance of the kingdoms of God. Luke 4:18 (NKJV) says, "The Spirit of the Lord *is* upon Me, Because He has anointed Me To preach the gospel to *the* poor; He has sent Me to heal *the* brokenhearted, To proclaim liberty to *the* captives And recovery of sight to *the* blind, *To* set at liberty those who are oppressed." Jesus anoints us to do the Father's will.

The sixth takeaway was that I did not lose my faith in the valley of the shadow of death; in fact, I clung to the truth that **God is good all the time.** Psalm 107:1 (NKJV) says, "Oh, give thanks to the Lord, for *He* is good! For His [lovingkindness] *endures* forever." Thankfulness helped me get through many of those very dark days; thankfulness and believing I would see the goodness of God. Psalm 27:13 (NKJV) says, "*I would have lost heart, unless I had believed That I would see the goodness of the Lord In the land of the living.*" The truth is that God is good all the time. "Oh, taste and see that the Lord is good; Blessed is the man who trusts in Him!" (Psalm 34:8, NKJV). Believe, taste and see!

The seventh takeaway is **that obedience is the key to life.** Surrender and obedience go together like peanut butter and jelly. Obeying the Word of God comes out of a surrendered life; a heart for Jesus. To obey and surrender are daily choices. You can choose of the path of life or the path leading to death. James 4:7 (NKJV) says, "Therefore submit to God. Resist the devil and he will flee from you." The Lord reached down into the pit I was in and breathed life into me. In that moment, His breath brought strength, and I heard His voice. He wanted me to obey His voice. The Lord could have healed me completely on that day as I was laying down, desperately crying out with my whole being, but He had me obey His voice before the full healing came. Obedience is vital. Obedience is better than sacrifice. 1 Samuel 15:22 (NKJV) says, "Behold, to obey is better than sacrifice." Abraham demonstrated in Genesis 22:1-19 just how important obeying the voice of the Lord truly is for all. Obedience brought Abraham's provision, and his own son was not sacrificed. The Lord provided the sacrifice. Abraham obeyed the Lord's voice, then provision and blessing came.

The eighth takeaway is that I found joy in the shadow of the valley of death. **I perceived the power of the Lord's presence and clearly saw myself in the shadow of His wings more than I perceived the shadow of death.** Psalm 63:7 (NKJV) says, "Because You have been my help, Therefore in the shadow of Your wings I will rejoice." Every time I felt the Presence of God, His peace and strength would fill me even more. John 16:33 (NKJV) says, "These things I have spoken to you that in Me You may have peace. In the world you will have tribulation: but be of good cheer I have overcome the world." Jesus overcame! I had a choice to keep looking at the shadow of death or fix my eyes on Jesus and abide in the shadow of His wings. The fullness of joy is in the presence of God. Choosing His joy filled me to overflow with His strength and His peace to move on out of the valley of death. His shadow was actually light, a brilliant light that pierced the darkness and dispelled it out of my path.

The ninth takeaway is that **the words of life in Psalm 23 helped carry me through the valley.** There is no lack in God's kingdom. Jesus is my portion; He is all in all, He supplies everything I need and more. Under the shadow of His wing, He restored my soul. Psalm 23:4 (NKJV) says, "I will fear no evil; For You are with me." Knowing the Lord was with me, hiding me in the shadow of His wing, helped me see He prepared the way to lead me out of the valley. Obedience to the words Jesus spoke fueled the flame lighting the way out of the valley of the shadow of death. He anointed my head with His oil of joy as He wiped away all my tears. He is continually restoring, strengthening, filling, all for His good pleasure. The Lord comforts me with His peace if I choose to receive it, to receive Him, even when in distressing places. He leads me. When I choose His Word over all else, He leads me beside waters of rest. In the stillness, Jesus is there. It was in the stillness of waiting upon Him after I completely surrendered my will to His will while crying out to Him that I was comforted by Him, by His goodness. The Lord's goodness and mercy shall follow me all the days of my life. Psalm 23:6 (NKJV) says, "Surely goodness and mercy shall follow me All the days of my life: And I will dwell in the house of the Lord forever. All my days, even the years spent in the valley of the shadow of death, the goodness of God and His mercy have followed me."

The final takeaway is **that having a vision and spending time journaling with Jesus is vital.** Habakkuk 2:2 (NKJV) says, "And then the Lord answered me and said: 'Write the vision And make *it* plain on tablets, That he may run who reads it." Writing down the dreams, visions, and words on our hearts can give us a road map to achieve them. I am a grandma of nine grandchildren and did not believe I needed a vision. When I was in DI Ministry School, I thought it was a waste of time to write out a vision and mission statement. However, because I needed to have a vision and mission statement to complete the class, I said, "Fine. Lord, if You want me to have a vision, then reveal it to me, because I don't have one." Sure enough, the Lord dropped a vision and mission statement into me. He spoke four words: "Carry Presence Live Possible." In those four words was everything Jesus had done when He breathed life, strengthened, filled with joy, and raised me off the sick bed.

The first vision statement I wrote in May of 2019 fully came to pass with all the dreams and visions I had on it within one year. Now, I am on my second version of my vision statement and the dreams and visions are still becoming reality.

VISION STATEMENT
Carry Presence Live Possible

MISSION STATMENT
Staying in His presence and ushering in His presence. Daily living as proof that all things are possible. Demonstrating impossibilities made possible by God.

LIFE SCRIPTURES
These are the scriptures that breathe life into my being. I read them and declare them every day.

In Your presence *is* fullness of joy; At Your right hand are pleasures forevermore.

Psalm 16:11 (NKJV)

"Do not be afraid; only believe."

Mark 5:36 (NKJV)

I can do all things through Christ who strengthens me.

Philippians 4:13 (NKJV)

The LORD is my shepherd; I shall not [want]. He makes me to lie down in green pastures; He leads me beside the still waters.

He restores my soul; He leads me in the paths of righteousness

For His name's sake. Yea, though I walk through the valley of the shadow of death, I will fear no evil; For You are with me;

Your rod and Your staff, they comfort me. You prepare a table before me in the presence of my enemies; You anoint my head with oil; My cup runs over. Surely goodness and mercy shall follow me All the days of my life; And I will dwell in the house of the LORD Forever.

Psalm 23:1-6 (NKJV)

He who is in you is greater than he who is the world.

1 John 4:4 (NKJV)

Jesus said, "it is finished!" And bowing His head he gave up his Spirit.

John 19:30 (NKJV)

I would have lost heart, unless I had believed that I would see the goodness of the Lord in the land of the living.

Psalm 27:13 (NKJV)

But Jesus looked at them and said to them, "With men this is impossible, but with God all things are possible."

Matthew 19:26 (NKJV)

Because You have been my help, Therefore in the shadow of Your wings I will rejoice.

Psalm 63:7 (NKJV)

Rejoice always, pray without ceasing,

1Thessalonians 5:16-17 (NKJV)

DAILY ACTIONS

- Absolute surrender and communion with Jesus, fostering an atmosphere for His presence.

- Carry His presence twenty-four-seven and usher in king Jesus everywhere I go.

- Declarations: to *speak out what is seen*; speak as though it already is. "God, who gives life to the dead and calls those things which do not exist as though they did" (Romans 4:17, NKJV). Declare over self, family, region, nation, all things the Lord shows, declare it. Declare Your Lovingkindness in the morning and Your Faithfulness by night (Psalm 92:2 NKJV).

GOALS

I have two-year, five-year, and ten-year goals written down to look at and pray into them every day. The Lord puts desires in our hearts and He is so faithful to breathe life into our dreams and visions. Psalm 37:5 (NKJV) says, "Commit your way to the Lord, Trust also in Him, And He shall bring it to pass."

JOURNALING

Journaling each day is just as important as looking at a vision and mission statement every day. Journaling or talking to God through writing has been pure joy since coming out of the valley. Journaling helped me process all the keys God gave me while in the valley of the shadow of death. From time to time, I read through all the words the Lord had spoken to me. When I look back at my journals, I see how faithful the Lord has been my entire life.

Daily Journal Entry:

- **Word:** Ask, pray, listen, receive the Word, and write the word or words down. Write out any impressions and listen.
- **Scripture:** Look up the scriptures for the Word or words received and write them down. Meditate on the Word. Lean into the Lord's presence. He is the Word!
- **Application/Takeaway:** Write out any reflections/impressions from waiting on the Lord, meditating on the Word given, and how will you act on the Word. That is the application of the day's daily bread. In this manner, we walk out how The Lord desires us to carry *His presence* and *live possible* with the fresh manna for that day.

This is a page from my journal in early 2020. This format is how I talk with the Lord every day. He speaks, and I write it down, look up the scriptures that resonate; then I meditate, ask questions, and lean into His presence.

JOURNAL ENTRY from
March 24, 2020

Words from God	Impressions
Rise up.	Time to get moving
Rise up out of the saunter.	Move out of idealness
Come.	An invitation to come into His presence
I say, 'Come unto me.'	The Lord wants deeper communion
Bring hope.	We carry our king Jesus everywhere 247.
Carry hope.	The Lord wants us to intentionally carry His light of hope
Bring hope to the hopeless.	The Lord is calling us to bring hope to the dark places

Open the prison doors.	Open the prison doors of the mind
Set the captives free.	By faith, He moves through us in power to set the captives free

Scriptures

Isaiah 61 and focus on verses 1-3.

Isaiah 35 and focus on verses 3-4.

Takeaway

Sense that the Lord is calling us, His body, to deep communion at this hour. It's time for us to be fully positioned before Him with eyes, ears, and hearts fixed on Him so that He will pour out His Spirit through us to bring His light into the darkness, hope to the hopeless, will set the captives free, and fill His people with His joy!

Journaling Summary:

This journaling process is a constant dialogue. These three steps in my journaling process of writing down what the Lord is saying or showing me, lining it up with Scripture, meditating on the Word and writing out the takeaways helps me to position my heart to carry God's presence and live all things possible each day.

Finally, here are the **action steps** that I took in the valley of the shadow of death. The Lord walked me through the valley, but I had to take action to make it out to the other side. Reflecting on the long journey through the valley of the shadow of death, I encountered the living God who saturated me with His Presence, marked me with His Joy, and gave me a new lens to see His goodness. This process involved the following actions on my part.

Crying out: Ask, cry out, and seek Jesus.
"In my distress I called upon the Lord, And cried out to my God; He heard my voice from His temple, And my cry came before Him, *even* to His ears" (Psalm 18:6, NKJV).

Surrender: A one hundred percent surrender, not just ninety or ninety-nine percent; fully surrendering and desiring the Father's will, not my own will, but God's will be done. "Your kingdom come. Your will be done On earth as it is in heaven" (Matthew 6:10, NKJV).

Obey: Obey the Word. Obey the voice of God.
"But He said, 'More than that, blessed are those who hear the word of God and keep it!'" (Luke 11:28, NKJV).

Receive: Fully live by the Spirit of God drink Him in daily. "For by one Spirit we were all baptized into one body—whether Jews or Greeks, whether slaves or free—and have all made to drink into one Spirit" (1 Corinthians 12:13 NKJV).

Abide: Wait on the Lord; choose to remain in His presence, to invite the Lord into every area of life. Posture my heart towards the Lord and wait upon Him. Live each moment by the Spirit of God. "By this we know that we abide in Him, and He in us, because He has given us of His Spirit" (1 John 4:13 NKJV).

Walk it out: Carry presence, live possible. When I carry king Jesus everywhere, I live and demonstrate to others that all things are possible. "Jesus said to him, 'If you can believe, all things are possible to him who believes'" (Mark 9:23, NKJV). "'With men this is impossible, but with God all things are possible'" (Matthew 19:26, NKJV).

Prayer

Father, thank You for touching each person who read this book. Thank You for strengthening their innermost being. Thank You for releasing them from every stronghold in their mind. Thank You, Jesus, for flooding them with Your joy and peace and saturating them with Your love. Lord, remove each stumbling block and set them on the path of life that You have revealed to them by Your Spirit. All things are possible to those who believe, and we believe. Thank You, Lord Jesus, for releasing Your healing touch bringing freedom now, in Your mighty name, Jesus. Thank You, Lord Jesus; one touch from You changes everything! Amen.

Book Cover

Artwork by Yonnah Ben Levy

Yonnah Ben Levy was raised in Seattle and Mercer Island. She attended Whitman College and received her B.A. in art from George Washington University in Washington, D.C., where she studied painting and ceramics at the Corcharan Gallery. Yonnah received a Masters of Art for Teachers at the University of Washington. She has been a professional artist since 1976. Her bronze sculptures and paintings of wildlife and birds have been exhibited in galleries and museums such as the Museum of Native American Art in Spokane. In 1981, she made "Aliyah" and worked for artists and craftsmen in various media, including illuminated parchments, ceramics, jewelry, woodcarving, and sculpture. Since 1989, she has been collaborating with her husband, Chaim Bezalel, on their own original work under the combined signature, Bezalel-Levy. She also continues to pursue her own sculpture and ceramic work. She taught art in the Israeli school system for ten years. In 1998, she returned to America and established Stanwood House Gallery and Art Center in Stanwood, where she continues to teach and produce paintings, sculptures, and ceramics.

End Note

This picture is of my COVID-19 antibody test result. It demonstrates that I had COVID-19 and developed antibodies to COVID-19. This is another miracle! Not only did I not feel sick when I had COVID-19 (no fever, no fatigue; nothing except losing my sense of smell and taste briefly back in September), but my immune system worked perfectly and created antibodies—specifically IGG—for COVID-19. In the past, I was given IGG infusions twice a month because my body was not producing them to fight off viruses and infections due to CVID (combined variable immunodeficiency), but God! The Lord healed me, including the invisible disease the doctors diagnosed, and my body is now creating antibodies without medical intervention.

About the Author

Lisa Lancaster, founder of Carry Presence Live Possible, lives in the Pacific Northwest on a small scenic farm with her husband, Jeff. She and Jeff have five wonderful children and nine grandchildren. She earned a teaching certificate and graduated Cum Laude from Western Washington University after returning to school while raising her children. Lisa has served many years in missions and as a Sunday school teacher. She enjoys hosting family gatherings, cooking, writing, photography, gardening, and traveling to India.

To learn more, visit:

Website: www.carrypresencelivepossible.com
Instagram: @CarryPresenceLivePossible
Facebook: Carry Presence Live Possible

Website: www.impactasiainternational.org
Instagram: @impact.asia
Facebook: Impact Asia International